# Leave it to God

by

Brian Humek

# Other Books by Brian Humek

Non-Fiction

**Drop**: A realistic look at spirituality from the inside out

**Purple Ducks**: Reflections on why in the world we need to belong

Fiction

**Summer of Sharona**  (YA Novel)

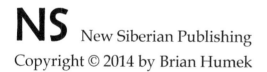 New Siberian Publishing

# Dedications

I first of all thank God for giving Joe Connelly and Bob Mosher the genius to create a beloved television show like *Leave it to Beaver*.

I thank my father Tom Humek for his constant support of all my endeavors. Without his encouraging words and all the other ways he has helped, this project wouldn't have happened. I thank my mom for giving me a love for God and my wife and son for enduring with me as I researched and wrote this book.

Thanks go out to my friends, teachers and ministers in the churches of Christ who have helped my faith grow over the many years of my Christian life and to all other ministers and church leaders I have come to know through my devotionals, Facebook groups or by meeting them in person.

# Table of Contents

# Introduction

My fascination with *Leave it to Beaver* began before I ever saw a single episode of the classic TV situation comedy. In the early 1980s, Charlie Rose had an interview program on CBS he filmed each day which aired from 2:00 a.m. to 6:00 a.m. On one particular morning, somewhere between those early morning hours, I watched an interview with two child actors, now grown up. Their names were Jay North who played *Dennis the Menace*, a show I watched frequently and the other actor was Jerry Mathers who everyone now knows as "The Beaver" from the situation comedy *Leave it to Beaver*, a show I had never seen.

I watched the interview and while the questions were basically the same for each actor, their answers were polar opposites. From Jay North, the answers spewed from his mouth with a big dose of bitterness as an exclamation point at the end of each sentence. However, from Jerry Mathers, the answers gently streamed, like the water of a babbling brook flowing into Friends Lake, and a smile accompanied each answer. The difference between the two actors was life changing for me.

After this evening of hearing Jay North complain about how sailors made fun of him while he was in the Navy and all the other trials and travails that happened upon him simply because he was cast as *Dennis the Menace*, I rarely if ever watched his program via reruns again. Seriously, one watches a show filled with innocent child characters because of the fun involved in their on screen ordeals and how the problems were solved. Isn't watching TV, especially classic comedies, supposed to be fun? Watching Jay North, a bitter man in his 30s who had no good memories of *Dennis the Menace* and who did nothing but complain about his experience would make watching the show a reminder of all the complaints I had heard spouted by Jay North. Life should be fun so right then, I became a *Leave it to Beaver* fan and never turned back.

Only recently, did I find out that Jay North, with the help of a therapist in the 1990s, finally came to terms with his early fame and the abuse he endured from his Aunt and Uncle because of it. My sincerest prayers go out to Jay and his family.

After that Charlie Rose interview, I soon found *Leave it to Beaver* on Superstation WTBS. Every week day, I watched both episodes that aired from 4:05 p.m. to 5:05 p.m. central time. As I watched the episodes and the silly situations Beaver found himself a part of, I did sometimes think back on that interview and the great amount of positivity Jerry Mathers exuded while speaking with interviewer Charlie Rose. These episodes I watched were a week in the life of Jerry Mathers. He had fun making these shows. They weren't his real life, but they were real life situations which happened to Richard Connelly, the eight year old son of show co-creator Joe Connelly. If the situations didn't happen to Richard or Joe Connelly's older boy Jay, they were taken from the real lives of other writer's kids.

I have never stopped marveling at Jerry Mather's attitude about *Leave it to Beaver*. Interviewers and authors are often amazed that he has kept such a positive attitude about his role in this classic TV comedy that first aired over 57 years ago. As I was putting the finishing touches on this book, I watched one last interview with Jerry, this one with Ken Boxer from February 2014. In the interview, Ken asked Jerry about the pluses and minuses of portraying Beaver Cleaver. Of course, Jerry rattled off as many pluses as he could in the limited time he had. Then again, Ken asked him to list some of the negatives. Jerry told him he hasn't found any negatives yet but if he does, he'd make sure to come back and let him know.

For Jerry, he may wonder why any actor would not revel in the fact that they are known all around the world and that people love the entertainment he or she helped bring into their homes in the 1950s and still today. "Why..." Jerry may ask, "...would I ever be unhappy about that?" If I am right about what Jerry thinks about his fame, something he has pretty much stated outright in numerous TV interviews, I think we have an outstanding mother to thank for his great attitude. No, that wouldn't be June Cleaver, even though she modeled that great attitude too, but the credit should go to Jerry's real mother and father. His parents raised him correctly.

Every interview and every interaction Jerry Mathers has with the press about his *Leave it to Beaver* days proves he has the attitude Christians should portray to the world. Whether or not Jerry Mathers is a Christian, or just played one on TV when we would see him arrive home from Sunday school or preparing to go to it, or those moments when he may mention God or the Bible, does not matter when it comes to the content of this book. *Leave it to God* is not endorsed by Jerry, Tony, or anyone else on the show. Everyone knows *Leave it to Beaver* demonstrates morals and good living and that is perfect to inspire devotionals for Christians in order to help them live better lives.

The actor who portrayed Ward Cleaver, Hugh Beaumont, was a lay Methodist minister and went into acting to help pay the bills while he ministered to others. I think things have worked out for the best. His flock may have eventually lost a minister due to his busy acting schedule, although he preached on occasion during the run of *Leave it to Beaver*, he is still helping minister to others through this book of devotionals.

I praise God for everyone associated with getting *Leave it to Beaver* on the air and for that desire in American TV audiences for not allowing it to leave the airwaves since its debut in 1957. And by the way, proof of my *Leave it to Beaver* fascination was found recently in an old journal entry I read from when I was unemployed and being a slacker in my early 20s, "Woke up at 1 p.m. watched *Leave it to Beaver*." This wasn't just one journal entry; it was basically a few months worth of journal entries. Now with Netflix, I can still record such journal entries, no matter what time I wake up these days.

The devotionals in this book are not all the same. Some talk about Beaver way more than they speak about God. Others are vice versa and speak about God in much more depth than Beaver. There are even a couple devotionals in which I stand up on a stage and preach. I ask your forgiveness for those.

Brian Humek
(A Leave it to Beaver addict who is not searching for a 12 step program)

## The Beginnings of Beaver

It may surprise fans of *Leave it to Beaver* to learn that the two men who produced this beloved portrayal of the traditional nuclear family, Joe Connelly and Bob Mosher, which airs around the world in over 90 different languages, were each raised in a broken home[1].

Joe Connelly and Bob Mosher as youngsters knew little of what they portrayed in the series as they grew up in New York City and Auburn, NY respectively during the 1920s. Their experience with the nuclear family came from their own marriages 25 years later. Mosher had two children and Joe Connelly had his quiver full with six children. The stories from their lives, and those of other writers, were the basis for all *Leave it to Beaver* episodes. In fact, Connelly's sons Ricky (age 8) and Jay (age 14) were the inspirations behind the roles of Beaver and Wally. [2]

The great writing/production team of Joe Connelly and Bob Mosher first met while working together at the J. Walter Thompson advertising agency in New York City about 1939. After striking a good friendship centered on creativity, the two left the agency in 1942 to take a job in Hollywood writing for the *Edgar Bergen/Charlie McCarthy Show*. Bob left first, Joe followed soon after. The team was soon in popular demand, following up their success on the Bergen/McCarthy show with writing stints for *The Phil Harris Show* (Jack Benny's Orchestra leader who teamed up with wife Alice Faye) and *The Frank Morgan Show*. The writing team then hooked up with *Amos 'n' Andy* stars Charlie Correll (the father of Beaver actor Richard Correll) and Freeman Gosden and wrote over 1500 shows for that series on radio and later on television. [3]

---

[1] Gerard Jones, *Honey, I'm Home: Sitcoms Selling the American Dream* (New York: St. Martins, 1992), 125.

[2] Dennis McLellan, Joe Connelly, 85; Helped Create 'leave It to Beaver.', *Los Angeles Times*, February 14, 2003.

[3] Stephen Cox, *The Munsters: A Trip Down Mockingbird Lane* (New York: Back Stage Books, 2006), 41.

After *Amos 'n' Andy*, the duo had two writing experiences which led them to believe that old axiom attributed to both William Faulkner and Mark Twain, "Write what you know." Their experiences were with a failed anthology series for actor Ray Milland and a successful movie screenplay for *The Private War of Major Benson*. The latter was a success because it was inspired by a real life event witnessed by Connelly as he drove one of his children to school. In their next situation comedy endeavor, they decided to follow the rule by writing what they knew. Connelly and Mosher were the fathers of nine children collectively, that was a lot of background material necessary for a situation comedy.[4]

Their new effort, *Leave it to Beaver*, the first family TV comedy to look at life though the eyes of children, debuted in October of 1957. The name "Beaver?" Well, it has been reported in many publications that "Beaver" was a nickname of a buddy of Connelly's while in the Merchant Marines. [5] So much for that disclaimer at the end of each *Leave it to Beaver* episode which states similarities to names or events in the show with real life individuals is simply a coincidence, right?

It was a sad day in American television history when the last episode of *Leave it to Beaver*, "Family Scrapbook" aired June 20, 1963. It ended a show of firsts with a first. Not only was it the first show in history to look at life though the eyes of a child character, it was also the first TV series to dedicate a final episode to closing out a series, as "Family Scrapbook" was a retrospective of the show's six years on the air. [6]

---

[4] McLellen, Dennis.

[5] Ibid.

[6] "Family Scrapbook: Trivia, Quotes, Notes and Allusions," tv.com, accessed September 29, 2014, http://www.tv.com/m/shows/leave-it-to-beaver/family-scrapbook-81230/trivia/.

## Purpose of this Book

The basic purpose of this book is to help Christians who love *Leave it to Beaver* to live lives more fully in tune to their Creator. Each devotional includes a prayer, a Bible passage (you'll need your own Bible to look it up) and a video clip time reference in case you are using this book as an aid for a small group or Sunday school lesson and would like to watch an appropriate video clip.

Although I hope Christians could use this book to enhance their spiritual life, there is a wider audience to be had by these devotionals inspired by *Leave it to Beaver* episodes. This book is also intended for anyone looking for God, whether that be for a first time encounter or for those looking for a deeper and more loving relationship. Even if someone hates God or doesn't believe in Him, but they love *Leave it to Beaver*, this book will entertain them.

This book has a little something for every *Leave it to Beaver fan*, those who are Christian and those who are not. If you simply love everything Beaver and could care less about the devotionals, check out the Season One Actor Encyclopedia included in the back of the book, including detailed biographies of the main actors and some who had recurring roles. You will also enjoy occasional "devotional breaks" which are filled with *Leave it to Beaver* trivia and tidbits, especially the Eight Great Eddie Haskell Season One Moments.

Christian or not, the morality and goodness of this classic television series resonates with people worldwide. I commend the producers, directors, writers, all other staff members, even that staff not mentioned in the credits and especially the beloved actors, for creating a timeless treasure that I watch way more often than I should, my family can attest to that, your family may say the same thing about you, right?

## For a Little While

Pilot "It's a Small World" April 23, 1957
Written by Joe Connelly and Bob Mosher
Bible Passage: James 4:13-15
Video Clip: 16:23 - 18:19

Prayer: *Dear God, help me do as much good as possible for the little time I am here in your world. Amen.*

There are three things I love most of all. They are God, my family and *Leave it to Beaver*. But of course, you must have known two of those three already because why else would I create a devotional book based on episodes of that iconic (boy, what an overused adjective) 1950s television series?

I love *Leave it to Beaver* to the point that I first began building up my collection of episodes by purchasing the DVD set for season one. As with all DVD sets, there is some special material included as a bonus. I absolutely loved the audio interview featuring Jerry Mathers and Frank Bank who respectively discussed their roles as Beaver and Lumpy on the television show. Another bonus on the DVD set is the pilot episode, "It's a Small World." This episode is not shown on TV along with the other 234 episodes.

As you may know, the pilot episode of a series is created to show network executives what a series will look like on the small screen. It also gives an opportunity for audiences to see it and their reactions are gauged. This helps networks decide whether to give a show the go ahead for production. Sometimes certain actors on a TV pilot will receive negative reviews and may be replaced with different actors. Maybe the plot will be modified and the show taken in an entirely different direction.

As for the pilot episode of *Leave it to Beaver*, you will notice two very big changes from the television series we all grew up to know and love. First of all, Ward Cleaver isn't really Ward Cleaver. Watching this pilot episode made me feel as if Martians had come down and replaced the body of Ward Cleaver with someone else. In fact, that's exactly what happened sans Martians. Ward Cleaver was portrayed by Max Showalter, not Hugh Beaumont. And lo and behold, this Ward Cleaver actually smoked in two different scenes of the show. It's not really explained anywhere why it happened, but the execs of the show decided to replace Showalter with Hugh Beaumont. Whewwww! What a relief!

Max Showalter didn't quit acting. He went on to do character acting in many roles for the next 27 years, up to his final appearance as Grandpa Fred in 1984's *Sixteen Candles*.

But what about that second big difference in the pilot? Well, that would be Wally Cleaver. He wasn't portrayed in the pilot by Tony Dow, the actor who played Wally for 234 episodes during the full run of *Leave it to Beaver*. Actor Paul Sullivan played Wally in the pilot episode. In my humble opinion, Paul wasn't a very good actor. There was no chemistry between him and his little brother. Can you imagine Paul's excitement when TV execs watched the pilot episode and green lighted the project to become a full fledged series? I can hear him now, running to his friends and saying, "I'm going to be co-starring on a television series. I'm going to be famous!" But wait… just before production was to begin on the show, Paul grew and grew and grew. He was quickly replaced with Tony Dow who happened to be in the right place at the right time. In fact, look up Paul Sullivan on the Internet Movie Database and you'll find a few more credits for him up until 1962 and then he simply disappears.

When reading the book of James, look what the author says about how we don't know anything about tomorrow. We're not guaranteed success in the business world or Hollywood for that matter. What are we according to James? We are just a mist that appears for a moment and then disappears. Here are James' words:

*Now listen, you who say, "Today or tomorrow we will go to this or that city, spend a year there, carry on business and make money." Why, you do not even know what will happen tomorrow. What is your life? You are a mist that appears for a little while and then vanishes. Instead, you ought to say, "If it is the Lord's will, we will live and do this or that."*

We sometimes get caught up in the rat race called life and forget to ask God to bless us in our endeavors and ask Him to help us accomplish the good things we'd like to do. But there are other times when we just neglect God and think we're doing all we do on our own, with no help from Him. He makes all things possible whether it's a Hollywood career, a business proposition, good grades in school or a relationship. We need God in all of these areas of our life and remember, we're just here for a little while and then we're gone. We should do good while we are here because the only thing that will last beyond our life span is the memories people have of our temporary mist like existence.

**Worry**

Episode 1 "Beaver Gets 'Spelled" October 4, 1957
Written by Joe Connelly and Bob Mosher
Bible Passage: Matthew 6:25-33
Video Clip: 4:43- 8:09

*Prayer: Dear God, If in your heavenly wisdom, you believe I worry too often, please help me rely only on you and to reap the benefits of a worry free life. Amen*

As a child, one of the most feared things in the world is to have a teacher give you a note to take home to your parents. This is exactly what happens on this episode of *Leave it to Beaver*. What did Beaver do? Did he pull Judy Hensler's pigtails? Did he get into a fight with Whitey Whitney? Was it that spit ball he blew at a Larry during lunch?

When given the note, Beaver seems to have no worries until Judy and Whitey inform him how bad it is to have a teacher send a note home. As their talk continues, Whitey tells Beaver about a boy who was expelled after taking a note home. Then Judy adds, "I bet you're gonna get it. They'll throw you right out of school." It is only then, that Beaver begins to worry. All of his misdeeds come rushing back into his mind. He's worried, but later at home; his big brother has a solution. They will write a return letter to Miss Canfield explaining how the Beaver has already been punished for the bad he has done. Of course, this causes more confusion than clarity and Miss Canfield inquires of Mrs. Cleaver about her letter. Eventually, Beaver runs to the park and up into a tree to escape punishment from his father.

How often does life give you a "note from the teacher?" How often does life give you some problem or situation which has you worried from the moment it appears until somehow God reveals to you the situation isn't exactly as bad as you think it is going to be? Not to compare Wally Cleaver to Satan, but think about it, Satan is the one who tells us to worry, and Wally did his share of scaring Beaver with worry about that note. Satan then gets you in deeper trouble when you try to cure your bad situation with answers that may be ungodly and not worthy of someone who has declared their love for Christ.

As it turns out, Miss Canfield only wanted permission from Mrs. Cleaver for her son to be able to play Smokey Bear in a school play. That's the way it is with us sometimes. We experience a situation that on the surface looks bad, feels bad, sounds bad, but in the end is simply just another situation in our lives that God has covered.

## Unmet Expectations

Episode 2 "Captain Jack" October 11, 1957
Written by Joe Connelly & Bob Mosher
Bible Passage: Acts 3:1-10
Video Clip: 1:48 -4:30

Prayer: *Dear God, I need your constant help to react in a way pleasing to you when things do not go my way and my expectations are not met. Amen.*

Okay, think back over your life, have you ever experienced an episode of unmet expectations? Hundreds of times? Yeah, me too. But what about when you were a kid, did you ever send off for something you saw in the back of a comic book, like the machine that made money, the X-ray glasses, or the dreaded "surprise package" which because you were willing to gamble, the company was going to send you something worth way more than the seventy-five cents you needed to cough up?

Over the years, Beaver and Wally had a habit of sending away for items found in comic books. It all seemed to begin with their desire to have a real live alligator. After reading the ad, Wally exclaims, "A real 8 foot alligator for only $2.50?" He should've known it was too good to be true. I could understand Beaver getting fooled, but his older, wiser brother should have known better.

They get a note in the mail saying they have a package waiting for them at the post office. They rush down to claim the package and when they see it, the package is the size of a shoebox. "Maybe they send the food first," says Beaver. Wally replies with some wisdom, too little, too late, I think, "It can't be food, there's holes in the box."
To their surprise, they open the box and find the teeniest of alligators inside. It couldn't be any longer than eight inches. Talk about unmet expectations, this has got to go down in history as one of the biggest.

There are unmet expectations found throughout life. There once was a lame man begging for alms outside the Temple in Jerusalem who always expected the Jews to give him some money, maybe a shekel or a denarius. But since it was the duty of those visiting the Temple to give alms, the lame beggar's expectations weren't unsusual. Then, one day, he saw Peter and John approaching the Temple. Peter saw the man and said, "Look at us." The beggar's attention was grabbed. He gave Peter and John his undivided attention. He was expecting something from these men, maybe some silver or gold. But what does Peter say? "Silver or Gold we do not have...."

Hold up, wait a minute!!! No silver, no gold. I was expecting something, money, an offer of a place to live, maybe even a full size alligator, but at least something. Peter continues and tells the beggar, "... but what we do have, we give you in the name of Jesus of Nazareth." They heal the beggar. No longer is he lame. He can walk, dance, skip and jump. He's completely healed.

Sometimes our expectations are unmet. That happens because we live in a fallen world where we don't get everything we want. But think of a time in your life where your expectations were unmet, but in the end, things turned out better than you expected. That certainly was the case of the lame beggar.

As for Wally and Beaver, their alligator didn't magically transform into an eight foot long beast. Instead, they received the admiration of their father for doing a good job of taking care of their baby reptile. They showed their parents they were responsible. They found their alligator, "Captain Jack," a home in an alligator refuge in town. Who knew Mayfield was big enough to have its own alligator refuge?

Things can turn out better than we expect, but without our commitment to God, rarely if ever, can that happen.

**Revenge or Peace**

Episode 3 "The Black Eye" October 18, 1957
Written by Joe Connelly and Bob Mosher; Story by Rick Vollaerts
Bible Passage: Romans 12:17-18
Video Clip: 5:59-9:57

Prayer: *Dear God, I sometimes seek revenge, at least in a nominal way, against those who do me wrong. I sometimes need a reminder from you that I should live in peace. Amen.*

In today's world, if a kid comes home from school with a black eye, the first things some parents may do is call the police, hire a lawyer and sue the offending party, then sue the school and then possibly hire a publicist. But in the late 1950s, this just wasn't the case.

In "The Black Eye," Beaver comes home and tries to disguise his injury because he really didn't want his parents to know he got into a fight. If he had won the scuffle, maybe Beaver would have been proud and want to boast about his pugilistic efforts, but that didn't happen here. He was knocked in the eye and the fight was over. He never threw a punch.

Ward, a proud father, when he heard his youngest son was in a fight had one question to ask, "What does the other guy look like?" Beaver answers with a disappointing, at least to his father, "Alright." Ward's parental pride fell to the ground like a load of bricks. There was only one answer to solve this problem of hurt pride, boxing lessons.

Ward had a boxing dummy set up and taught his son the finer points of left jabs and right crosses. Even with the lessons, Beaver wasn't going to get a knockout anytime soon. The main point Ward wanted to impress upon his not so athletically inclined son was this, "When someone hits you, hit them back." He wanted his son to have revenge. He sent him out of the garage back to see the person who had been aggressive with him.

If it had been up to Beaver, he would've just left well enough alone. It was done. He had a black eye. It would eventually go away. He didn't want to get revenge, especially since the person who gave him the black eye was his classmate Veronica Rutherford, a GIRL!!!

How much better would our own lives be if we left well enough alone instead of always wanting to get revenge of some sort simply because of our hurt pride. I think about churches which split apart because of personality clashes. Such clashes always result in hurt pride; people leave, churches fall apart, the unchurched world sees that Christians can't even get along. Many more souls stay in a lost condition because of such situations. Drivers get killed because they have hurt pride and would rather run up on a bumper or brake real hard in front of a bad driver, etc., all because of wounded pride. It sometimes makes us feel better to get back at someone rather than back down and live in peace.

God doesn't call us to always be passive. But when it comes to things God would see as trivial such as bad drivers or hurt feelings at church or on the job, look for the peaceful way out. That's what God wants from us, peace, not strife. Even if someone does evil to us, God says don't repay evil with evil. That's saying a lot. If that's what God says about evil, imagine what he wants from us in our everyday lives where things just happen and we want to get back at the other person, such as a spouse when we have a fight or a bully down the street, or the bad driver who cuts us off in traffic.

If we seek peace instead of revenge, God will smile upon us.

**Judging Others**

Episode 4 "The Haircut"  October 25, 1957
Written by Bill Manhoff
Bible Passage: James 5:16
Video Clip: 15:45-16:48

Prayer: *Dear God, Please allow me to be a person who loves more than I judge others and praise more than I condemn. Amen.*

If James Bond was given a mission and repeatedly could not accomplish it, do you think his superiors would give him the same mission again, for maybe a fifth or sixth chance at failure? He would have probably exhausted his opportunities. When you have a child who keeps messing up a mission, maybe it is keeping his room clean, sharing his toys or eating all his peas, we continue to let him keep trying. But if his failure was money related, such as losing it continually, when would you stop giving him or her chances? Would the threshold have to reach $10, $50 or maybe $100?

In this episode of *Leave it to Beaver*, June is surprised and a little bit upset that Ward gives Beaver money for a haircut and allows him to walk across town with it, seeing that he has lost a lot of money lately. But Ward wants to give him another chance to prove he's a responsible boy. Well, needless to say, he loses this money also. Not only does he lose it, he tries to cover up this latest loss and boy, does this cause a problem.

Beaver comes home and with Wally and his mom downstairs, he gives himself a hair cut to help cover up his problem of lost money. Wally soon discovers that once again, his little brother has lost money their parents had given him and he also discovers Beaver's self-inflicted hair cut. Wally convinces Beaver, as if he needed convincing, that he was in big trouble now. Being the nice brother he is, Wally agrees to help Beaver by finishing the bad haircut with hopes of making Beaver look more presentable. As you can imagine, that was an even bigger mistake. Now, this problem haircut needs to be covered up and the only idea they come up with is stocking caps. Yes, they tell their parents they cannot take off the stocking caps, even at the dinner table because if they did, they would not be allowed in a secret club since wearing stocking caps was their initiation.

That evening, while the kids are sleeping, June takes off Beaver's stocking cap. She lets out an audible gasp while surprisingly; she does not wake up her son. She's shocked to find what she has found. Someone has butchered her son's hair. Really, all that's happened is her son has messed up, big time, twice in the same day.

Has the same thing ever happened to you? Think about church for a moment, this happens in the Lord's church, probably more often than we'd like to admit. We see someone quite regularly. They seem like good normal church people; they don't seem to have many problems. Their kids behave. They aren't very needy in any way whatsoever. But deep down inside, their family is messed up. They make mistakes or commit sins quite often. The thing is, you just don't know about it. Then one day, they decide to take the "confess to one another" passages seriously and confess to you or a small group and you are utterly shocked. You actually let out a small audible gasp or something similar which shows your surprise or your disdain. Yes, this happens. Just ask someone you know who used to go to church. This may be the reason why they don't attend any longer.

Let's not be shocked when our friends, co-workers, fellow church members take off their own stocking caps and reveal their butt ugly hair, or maybe it's a mask they're wearing and they don't have money for makeup. Let's not gasp audibly. Let's hug visibly. Let's love and comfort and live out what those "confess to one another" verses really mean. James didn't want people to confess and be condemned. He wanted people to confess, be prayed for and become stronger Christians.

.

## Jealousy

Episode 5 "New Neighbors" November 1, 1957
Written by Joe Connelly and Bob Mosher
Bible Passage: James 3:16
Video Clip: 4:09-6:29

Prayer: *Dear God, I pray that I can find satisfaction in the possessions and relationships I have and that I will never long for those things or people who do not belong to me. Amen.*

Jealousy is a sin, but the world looks at being jealous differently, depending on the object of one's jealousy. My neighbor recently bought a new car, one that looks good, is thrifty on gas and doesn't break down. Those are all things I would like in a car, but don't have. I could be jealous but the thought has never really crossed my mind (until now). This would be a form of jealousy that for the most part would not cause harm. It would never elicit the type of passion that would have me in a rage, possibly killing the neighbor so I could take his car. There'd be no plotting of a death so I can somehow get his car. There has probably never been a plotline on any Law & Order episode for something so preposterous.

On the other hand, if my neighbor had a beautiful wife and I spent a lot of time with her, his passions may rise to a level that jealousy could cause my own death, or maybe my jealousy about his wife could have me rub him out somehow. Now that's a plotline you've seen many times on Law & Order, CSI, or any other prime time crime show.

It's unlikely Theodore "Beaver" Cleaver could elicit feelings of rage in a new neighbor. But thanks to Eddie Haskell with some help from Wally, the duo gives Beaver "the business" and that's exactly what Beaver believes might happen after he takes a bouquet of flowers to the wife of a new neighbor. Yes, Beaver did something innocent when he took her flowers at his mother's behest. As a gesture of gratitude, the new neighbor, Mrs. Donaldson, bends over and gives Beaver a kiss. Back home, Eddie confronts Beaver. "What were you doing over there?" he asks. "Took her flowers," answers Beaver. "No, we saw you kissing her," says Eddie. Beaver tries to deny it by telling Eddie that she was kissing him, not the other way around. Eddie warns Beaver about jealous husbands. Just like in the movies, Beaver may just wind up dead on account of the kiss.

Eddie Haskell was correct. The movies are now, and were then, filled with jealous husbands and subsequent murders. That even happens in real life, just set a Google alert for "jealous husband" and watch what pops into your inbox. Movies haven't changed a lot over the years either, just check out the Lifetime Movie Network some day.

Jealousy at whatever level is a bad thing because God wants us to be satisfied with what we have. He doesn't want us to be jealous of others and their possessions. God also doesn't want us to love our possessions more than we love Him. If we do that, we could get to the point where our jealousy could put us into a rage. Additionally, God definitely doesn't want us to spend so much time with other people's possessions where it causes jealousy on their part. So, the way we should live is this, don't be jealous of what other people have and don't do anything to cause others to be jealous.

Beaver wound up spending a few days in fear of Mr. Donaldson His fear was tremendously painful and the miscommunication could have caused a rift in the neighbor to neighbor relationship if not resolved, which it was. An agreement came to be that Beaver could kiss Mrs. Donaldson anytime he wanted, which Beaver swore would never happen again.

## For the Bible Tells Me So

Episode 6 "Brotherly Love" November 8, 1957
Written by Joe Connelly and Bob Mosher; Story by Norman Tokar
Bible Passage: 1 Timothy 3:16-17
Video Clip: 3:05-6:22

Prayer: *Dear God, I struggle mightily in life, sometimes more often that I would like to admit. Help me see the answers to my problems in your word and implement them in my life. Amen.*

Has anyone ever broken an agreement? Of course, the answer is a resounding "yes." Even contracts are broken each and every day. I think that's why there are so many lawyers in the world. Someone has to help people sue one another.

Think about peace agreements that have been put down in writing, they have quite often been broken before a lasting peace is established. This can be documented over the centuries. Just because things are written down does not mean people will believe in those words or live them out.

Wally and Beaver are a perfect example in the episode "Brotherly Love." Instead of exemplifying the title of this episode, they do exactly the opposite, much to the chagrin of their mother June. She is dismayed that Ward accepts the constant fighting and bickering. He basically tells June to just get over it. This was all a part of growing up, he said. June was having none of that. She was going to have them write up a friendship pact and make them sign it. She would show them how brothers are supposed to act and she'd have it in writing.

All seemed good for a couple days but then again their relationship blew up and finally June realized that her idea had not been a good one. She could not force Wally and the Beav to be friends 100% of the time.

Sometimes Christians think because something is written down that everyone else in the world will simply go, "Hey, it says in the Bible I should go to church," or "God's word says love my neighbor." Then, like these people have taken a magic pill, they go to church or love their neighbors. Things are not always that easy.

While the Word of God is powerful, we should be careful not to assume that just because it is filled with wise words that are good to adhere to and necessary to adhere to for salvation, that all we have to do is read the Bible and be perfect people. It doesn't even work that way with Christians who love God's word.

At one point in my life, I was struggling with a big spiritual problem and I mentioned this to an elder at the church I attended. He asked, "What does the Bible say about that?" I told him the appropriate answer and he said, "Just do what it says in the Bible." Maybe he was a bit like June Cleaver and didn't understand that reading some words on a piece of paper does not change our inner thoughts, desires, and predilections to be selfish. If it did, the world would be filled with perfect Christian zombies.

What June Cleaver found out was that young boys are filled with free will and you know what, so are you and I. We need to be guided by words written on paper, but our relationship with God needs to go so much deeper than that. Start today. Get down on your knees. Spend quiet time with God, both in His word and in your heart. You may just see the spiritual benefits of a deeper relationship with your maker.

**Be Shrewd**

Episode 7 "Water, Anyone?" November 15, 1957
Written by Clifford Goldsmith
Bible Passage: Matthew 10:16
Video Clip: 10:44-13:44

Prayer: *Dear God, Help me to know the importance of being both shrewd and innocent and to know the absolute correct time to combine both of these traits.*

If only one personality trait could be attributed to Beaver, that would be innocence. He is as innocent as a sheep or in his case, innocent as a little lamb.

Our Bible verse speaks of sending sheep out among the wolves and in the first season of *Leave it to Beaver*, who are the wolves? We'd all agree Eddie Haskell is one of the wolves. He's the alpha of the group. His fellow pack members are Chester, Tooey and Lumpy and sometimes Wally. Of course, none of those kids are evil incarnate, but in the way they treat Beaver sometimes, evil is not an adjective that is way off the mark.

In this episode, innocent Beaver wants to join the gang's baseball team. They are going to buy uniforms and if Beaver wants to be part of it, Wally says he'll have to earn the money for a uniform himself. Not finding any jobs he could do, Beaver becomes wise as a serpent and actually sells water to all the boys as they do the jobs their parents have given them on this Saturday afternoon. At first, Beaver is unsuccessful at selling water because why pay for it from a kid with a bucket when it's available right inside the house from the kitchen faucet? But soon after his failed attempts at being a water salesman, Beaver finds out from the water department crew that the water will soon be shut off for a couple hours during the middle of a dreaded heat wave. After the shut off, Beaver's water sales career skyrockets, albeit, to the chagrin of parents of the kids to whom he sells water.

Beaver is living out the rule to be wise or shrewd as a serpent and gentle as a dove. His customers claim Beaver is being mean and being a cheat to do his selling. However, he is being gentle as he does so, insisting all the time that he's simply a businessman trying to earn money. He could've charged so much more for the water, but didn't.

We, as Christians, will be persecuted in so many ways. In America, these methods of persecution will be more subtle than say in Iraq or other Muslim countries where Christians are crucified and kidnapped and butchered. However, we will still face some persecution and Jesus warned us about that in the book of Matthew. That's why he said we need to be wise or shrewd as the King James Version translates the Greek word *pronimos*.

Combining just the right amount of wisdom along with gentleness will get us a long way, whether we are trying to run a business or attempting to evangelize our friends, neighbors or relatives. We must be careful in the way we act because the world is against Christians. Don't develop a martyr complex, but simply live out your life the way God would want and help others come to know Him.

# BEAVER TIDBIT

## Religion and America's Favorite Family Situation Comedy

During the 1950s, religion was still a very large piece of the fabric that made up American life. Between 1955-1958, a time that encompassed the first two seasons of *Leave it to Beaver*, about half of Americans were attending church, that was the largest percentage of Americans up to that time to ever attend church, [7] a percentage that has steadily declined ever since. Church attendance was nearly 50% then and religion was not the dirty word it has become in the 21st century.

*Leave it to Beaver* was not overtly religious, but it didn't shy away from using God's name in a positive light. While the religious feelings are not known about many of its cast members, it is highly doubtful that any of them were anti-religious or atheists at the time of the show's filming. The producers and writers occasionally inserted religious references into episodes, whether it was church attendance of the family, especially that of the children, or references to God being all knowing and all seeing.

In season one, the boys are seen getting ready to attend Sunday school with Eddie Haskell in "Tenting Tonight." One would be within the bounds of logical questioning to ask, "What did Eddie Haskell learn at Sunday school?" His character certainly did not demonstrate many obvious Christian behaviors, especially those traits of integrity (Titus 2:7) or sincerity (2 Corinthians 2:17). In the episode "Beaver's Old Friend," Ward and June come home from church while Wally, Beaver and Eddie stay after for Sunday school. In "Beaver's Bad Day," there is a deep discussion about God in a little conversation between Beaver and his mom.

---

[7] Carol Tucker, "The 1950s – Powerful Years for Religion," USC News, June 16, 1997, accessed September 20, 2014, http://news.usc.edu/25835/The-1950s-Powerful-Years-for-Religion/.

Of the actors on the show, this is what is known about their religiosity. Hugh Beaumont (Ward Cleaver) was a lay minister in the Methodist Church. He graduated from the University of Southern California with a Masters in Theology. He played a minister, pastor, priest, reverend or chaplain ten times in his career on the small and large screen. [8] During his time on *Leave it to Beaver*, some of his Sunday mornings were spent preaching at local Methodist churches. [9]

Jerry Mathers came from a conservative Catholic upbringing[10] and was also a product after *Leave it to Beaver*, of Notre Dame High School, a parochial school in Sherman Oaks where his father was once a coach. Jerry has also done fundraising for Catholic education. He was the keynote speaker two years ago for the 16th Annual Bishop's Dinner for Catholic Education in his home town of Sioux City, Iowa.[11] Jerry, whether or not he is a devout Christian today, something we do not know since that is a very personal matter, does display Christian traits. The morality by which he lives his everyday life and his positive attitude demonstrated in numerous interviews, both reflect how Christians should behave.

However, back in 1957 we do know this about Jerry Mathers, he said bedtime prayers each night. One day, he worked with Hugh Beaumont on a short commercial film. Hugh played Jerry's father in the short. Jerry and his mother enjoyed working with Hugh that day. Jerry's mother Marilyn had told Hugh about auditions for the role of Ward Cleaver on a show which had been purchased by CBS. They needed someone to replace the actor who had portrayed

---

[8] "Hugh Beaumont," IMDB.com, accessed September 22, 2014, http://www.imdb.com/name/nm0064604/.

[9] Barbara Billingsley, interviewed by Karen Herman, Santa Monica, CA, July 14, 2000.

[10] Tony Dow, interviewed by Eric Greenburg, October 6, 2006.

[11] Renee Webb, "Jerry Mathers Keynotes Bishop's Dinner," Catholic Globe, October, 2012, accessed September 21, 2014, http://www.catholicglobe.org/Renee10.18.12b.html.

Jerry's father in the pilot. That evening, Jerry said his usual prayers, but added this specific request, "Please God, make the actor I worked with today my father in the new series." A couple months later, Jerry and his mother saw God in action when they walked onto the *Leave it to Beaver* set on day one and Hugh Beaumont greeted them. [12]

Of the other actors on the show that have mentioned religion or Christianity, been mentioned by others in the same context, or had a Christian education, there are a few. Among them are Pamela Beaird who played Wally's love interest Mary Ellen Rogers in quite a number of episodes. Years after the show, she went on to college and graduated from Southwestern Assemblies of God University. She's also had a daughter win accolades at another Christian university. Ken Osmond has always presented himself as a very moral man and Barbara Billingsley commented in her Archives of American Television interview that dinner at his house was preceded by Ken saying grace for those around the table. Something she mused was very un-Eddie like. [13] Stanley Fafara, after his battles with addiction ended, or possibly, because of it, declared his own dependence on Christ as his savior. [14]

There are three *Leave it to Beaver* episodes that come quickly to mind where God is spoken of directly They were, "Beaver's Bad Day," "Beaver and Kenneth," and "Beaver's Prize." On the latter episode, Larry and Beaver discuss with their child logic, some very deep theology on the workings of God. There were also many episodes that spoke of the family going to church or Sunday school. Sometimes the parents went too, but they would typically skip Sunday school which seemed to occur after worship as seen in "Beaver's Friend." At other times, the parents did not attend worship or Sunday school. Two episodes in which we see the boys

---

[12]    Marilyn Mathers, "My Mother's Memories of Hugh Beaumont...," jerrymathers.com, February 16, 2013, accessed September 10, 2014, http://www.jerrymathers.com/my-mothers-memories-of-hugh-beaumont/.

[13] Barbara Billingsley interviewed by Karen Herman.

[14] Stanley Fafara, emailed to Tim Schmitt, August 10, 1998.

leaving for or coming home from church are "Tenting Tonight" and "Beaver's Pigeons." In other episodes such as, "Wally's Haircomb," "Substitute Father," and "The Hypnotists," their attendance at Sunday school or church is spoken about. In "Beaver and Chuey," June talks about her not wanting Wally to beat up Eddie because as she says, "This is Sunday," a day she knew in her heart was a special day. In the episode, "Eddie's Double-Cross," Beaver talks to Wally about how tricky girls are and he relates to his brother the story about Samson and Delilah he had recently learned about in Sunday school.

While *Leave it to Beaver* was not a religious show in any sense of the term, the producers and writers were definitely not afraid of the Christian religion. That is to be applauded.

**Favoritism**

Episode 8 "Beaver's Crush" November 22, 1957
Written by Joe Connelly and Bob Mosher, story by Phil Leslie
Bible Passage: Galatians 3:26-29
Video Clip: 3:44-6:19

Prayer: *Dear God, Please help me be fair with all those I come into contact with each day. Allow no favoritism to escape my heart and help me see others as you see them.*

Being the teacher's pet in elementary school is not conducive to making friends, or keeping them. Beaver's crush on Miss Canfield has him doing nice things for her, collecting papers, cleaning erasers and anything else that would keep him near her. In return, she shows him some favoritism. The kids in class do not like what they perceive as Beaver being the teacher's pet. Larry Mondello and the other kids in class try to get Beaver to prove he's not the teacher's pet by having him stuff a spring action snake into her desk drawer. Reluctantly, Beaver agrees to do so, but the next morning, Miss Canfield discovers the snake and it never does pop out of her desk drawer, much to the disappointment of the students.

Favoritism can do damage in a lot of ways. While the Bible talks about how all are equal in God's eyes (Galatians 3:28), there are examples of favoritism in the Bible such as in the story of Joseph. He was the favorite of his father and having a big mouth didn't endear him to his eleven brothers. He said the following to his brothers, "Listen to this dream I had: We were binding sheaves of grain out in the field when suddenly my sheaf rose and stood upright, while your sheaves gathered around mine and bowed down to it." With the favoritism already shown by their father toward Joseph, add this dream and instant hatred, huh? You may know the rest of the story. They throw Joseph into an empty cistern and then sell him into slavery. They go back to their father and show him Joseph's bloody coat. Jacob believes he's been eaten by a ferocious animal.

Years later, through some marvelous events set into motion by God, Joseph is the de-facto leader of Egypt. He's Pharaoh's right hand man. His brothers wind up coming to him for help during the middle of a terrible famine.

I've not been anyone's favorite anything but I have seen favoritism in action. Just this past baseball season, I saw how favoritism can do damage. It all began the previous fall when a baseball coach spoke about "his kids." He meant the group of kids that were part of his spring baseball team in contrast with the extra kids, including my son and a few others who were now on his fall team. I never really noticed the dichotomy he mentioned until a fellow parent of one of the "other" kids brought it to my attention. It still didn't bother me. But Jake's parents were particularly upset about it and would do their best to start a team in the next spring session for their son and any others who wanted to belong. So, favoritism by the coach caused Jake's dad to want to become a coach himself. Unfortunately, I signed my son up to be on Jake's team for the next spring session. It was a disaster in many ways.

This new team had its own favored player. It was the coach's son. He wasn't a second basemen but he played there almost every inning of the season. Just like in the case of Beaver and the teacher, the favoritism shown Jake by his father did not do his son any favors. No one liked Jake. His attitude was bad and the team lost morale every time balls bounded by him or rolled under his glove or avoided his glove when they were thrown to him. It seemed as if his glove had some sort of cowhide repellant sprayed on it before each game. But there was that one time he accidentally caught a ball when by some miracle of God he was put in left field.

Favoritism never does anyone any favors. It didn't do Beaver a favor. He was made fun of for being the teachers' pet. It didn't do Joseph any good. He was sold as a slave. And favoritism didn't do Jake a favor. It merely gave him a false feeling of importance.

Let's do what God would want us to do, treat people fair and equal but not giving them a false sense of superiority, especially a kid. That tends to lead to nowhere but trouble when an adolescent reaches adulthood.

**Charity**

Episode 9 "The Clubhouse" November 29, 1957
Written by Connelly & Mosher; Story by Lydia Nathan
Bible Passage: Hebrews 13:16
Video Clip: 23:04-24:59

Prayer: *Dear God, Help me to do good for others, even offering charity, without first having to examine every single motive of those I may be inclined to help.*

On a rainy day, Beaver and Wally have nothing to do. Beaver suggests playing or trading marbles, but that idea is shot down. When Wally's friends arrive, they suggest the same thing and so they do it. While playing marbles, Beaver suggests they build a clubhouse, that idea is ignored until Eddie suggests it and so, after the rain, that's exactly what they do. There will be dues for anyone joining the club and 8th graders will be charged $1.00 and 2nd graders like Beaver will be charged $3.00 to join. That's when Beaver goes to work raising the money.

In the park, Beaver finds his inspiration in a down on his luck man named Pete who wears a sandwich board and charges for advertising. Beaver decides to do the same thing. Pete says he could make some money but he has to have a lot of inspiration to keep going instead of sitting down. Beaver creates his sign and after finding out the local bridge he spits off of, because he is a resident of the city, belongs to him; he decides to charge people ten cents to have the opportunity to spit off of it themselves.

Beaver rakes in the money and at the end of the afternoon, he's sitting on the same park bench where he first met Pete who soon arrives and sits down asking how well Beaver has done. Beaver counts his money and says he made $1.75. Pete sits down alongside Beaver and proceeds to tell him a sob story about his daughter Jasmine and how his family won't have anything to eat. Feeling bad for Pete and his family, Beaver, without much thought, turns over his hard earned cash so Jasmine could have some food for supper.

Have you ever heard a sob story? Have you or your church ever been taken by people you knew were telling you a tale so they could probably just go out and get another bottle of whiskey or buy cigarettes. Years ago, my wife used to work in our church food pantry. She would help dispense food to many people, some of which drove better cars than her, people she'd see smoking, families she knew to be lying because they discussed fake addresses right in front of her. She didn't argue with them about their right to receive food. She was there to give. But what is a person to do when it comes to those who ask for actual money from a church or an individual so they can get high or drunk?

Jesus said to feed the hungry and clothe those who need clothes and when we do it for them, we do it for him too. While there are some churches who give to those in need without any questions asked, there are others who have very strict guidelines on who they will help.

Our family has even needed help from time to time. One of the last situations was when we traveled to Wyoming from Texas to see my mom who had suffered a massive stroke and we had no money for gas. We contacted many churches to see which ones could help. Three offered help with no questions asked. One accused me of being a spammer and trying to rip them off and one said he needed more information because he had looked on my blog, Facebook and elsewhere and didn't find my announcing my need to the world or that I would soon leave my house for a week. Sorry people, I do not announce when and where I will be going out of town on social media.

So how should the church or individuals respond to pleas for help? Should we give the third degree or just give some of our resources like Beaver did? What do you or your church do when asked for handouts or help? What would Jesus want us to do?

Those are a lot of questions which sometimes elicit difficult answers. Prayer and diligent study of God's word will help us with the answers, hopefully in time before the next person, whose motives we may have doubts about, comes our way asking for help.

## Grubby Little Infants

Episode 10 "Wally's Girl Trouble" December 6, 1957
Written by Ben Gershman and Mel Diamond
Bible Passage: Mark 10:13-16
Video Clip: 16:20-17:00

Prayer: *Dear God, I need help from time to time in order to have a childlike faith. Please let joy, hope and faith as great as a child be part of my everyday life. Amen.*

There are times when little kids can be a pain in the neck. Admit it. If you have children, they aren't always little bundles of rainbows and sunshine. But you would never neglect them, never want to get rid of them, they are yours forever.

Some people in this world feel little Beaver Cleaver can be annoying or a pain in the neck. What are they talking about? He's adorable. Well, one such person was Penny Jamison, a girl Wally meets at dancing class on the day he and Beaver had agreed to ditch class and go fishing. Wally's new infatuation takes away all his thoughts of fishing. Not only does he forget about their immediate plans to fish, but Wally becomes consumed with Penny. Not until after Beaver does all of Wally's chores while he spends the afternoon with Penny, does Wally agree to take Beaver fishing the next day. A little guilt goes a long way.

Penny does not like Beaver or any "grubby infants" as she calls little kids like Beaver. She sounds a lot like the disciples when the little children were trying to see Jesus. Oh no, they couldn't let Jesus be bothered by little kids or "grubby infants" as Penny Jamison called them.

What does Jesus say about those kids? Not only did he say, "Stop the nonsense; let the little kids come to me!" He also told the disciples, "The kingdom belongs to such as these."

What Penny Jamison and others may disregard about little kids is their hearts, their innocence, their pure love. God wants to see us, even as adults, have a childlike innocence and a pure love. He understands that we'll all have entanglements that get us off the right path, but through Jesus, we can see our path corrected. If we're Christians and we miss the mark (sin), simply ask for the forgiveness God wants to give us. Children can have that pure love, pure heart and pure innocence which lasts for years on end. But there does come a time, and it is different for every human, when we'll need forgiveness. That's when we need Jesus most of all. We need him to help us get back to being those "grubby infants" with pure hearts we all used to be. We may have been grubby, but at least we loved with an undistracted heart.

The world is always a better place when we love with an undistracted heart.

**Come to My World**

Episode 11 "Beaver's Short Pants"   December 13, 1957
Written by Joe Connelly and Bob Mosher
Bible Passage: John 1:14
Video Clip: 21:22-23:49

**Prayer:** *Dear God, You have put me in other people's lives so I could be better able to show them you. Let my heart always be attuned to such opportunities when they arise.*

One of the unique things about *Leave it to Beaver* is that each episode's plot was true. The life situations of the writers and producers were worked into every episode. The producers and main writing team on the show, Bob Mosher and Joe Connelly, had nine children between them. The sad thing about the show, realizing all episodes are based on fact, is that some kid in the 1950s at age six had to wear short pants to school. Oh my, just watching Beaver's Aunt Martha taking him shopping for "short pants" and making him wear that geeky 19th century looking outfit to school hurt my heart. I hope you never had an Aunt Martha who did that or something similarly embarrassing to you.

So it's Monday morning and Aunt Martha is going to make Beaver wear his new short pants to school. You could imagine the results. Kids make fun of him. He gets into a fight and it's all Aunt Martha's fault. That's how Wally explains it to Ward.

Not about to let it happen again, Ward tells Wally that he'll take care of everything. Isn't that the same as how God says he'll take of everything? That's why fathers are in our lives, they are the living breathing love of God put into our lives for us to hold and be held by, embracing us in loving hugs, helping us to somehow better understand God's love for us, but in a tangible way. My heart hurts for those who have no earthly father for one reason or another.

But for us as humans to really identify with God, we needed something special to happen. That occurred when God came to earth as Jesus. He was born as a little baby in a manger and experienced everything we'd ever experience in this world, the hunger, the temptations, the pain.

Well, in this episode of *Leave it to Beaver*, this young boy of about seven years of age learned a very valuable and similar lesson as we learned from having Jesus come to earth. The next day arrives and Beaver is dressed in his ridiculous looking short pants outfit. Believe it or not, it came with a matching shirt, jacket, suspenders and hat. Beaver is scared because his dad is nowhere in sight. "Where's Dad?" he anxiously asks his brother. Wally tells him he's gone to work. Oh my, not again. What's going to happen? Will he ditch school today?

Well, Dad to the rescue. He sees Beaver leave out the back door and he calls out to him and motions him over to the garage. He gives Beaver some jeans and tells him he can just put them over the short pants and take off the silly looking jacket and replace it with his very own jacket he typically wore to school.

After he's put on the jeans and jacket and taken off the hat, Ward says, "Now, there's the old Beaver." His son looks at him with astonishment and proclaims, "Dad, you're just like one of the fellas." That's exactly what he was. Ward demonstrated to his son that he understood what he was going through and he actually had gone through something similar himself in his youth.

Ward Clever came to Beaver's world to show him he understood what he was going through as a kid. God did the same for us when he pitched his tent with us or moved into our neighborhood as one Bible translation puts John 1:14.

We should feel very special knowing God wanted to literally understand our world and our trials on a personal, not an otherworldly basis. And in that process, He suffered a most tortuous death, just for us. Thank you God!

**Paying Our Debts**

Episode 12 "The Perfume Salesmen"  December 27, 1957
Written by Mel Diamond and Ben Gershman
Bible Passage: Romans 4:25
Video Clip: 12:01- 13:38

Prayer: *Dear God, Open my heart to your love more and more each day. I need to trust you deeper and more fully than I do at this moment. Amen.*

Remember selling those World's Finest Chocolates as a kid? I think we've all done that. If we didn't sell them ourselves, we have sold them for our own kids at work or watched them sell those chocolate covered almonds or chocolate bars to church members on Wednesday nights or Sunday mornings. Selling whatever is just a part of growing up.

It's simple to sell chocolates. Everyone wants something delicious and fattening to eat. But what if what your child was trying to sell was some stinky perfume? How would you help them sell it?

Ward does it in "The Perfume Salesmen," with a little bit of trickery. His kids have sent away for some perfume to sell. It's called, "Flower of the Orient," but smells not like a flower, but like an old baseball glove. He takes a list of June's women's club members and calls each member, asking them to buy a bottle of the perfume and promises to reimburse them if they don't like it.

Not that selling perfume that smells like an old baseball glove is a sin, but think of the idea of having your sins reimbursed. Someone is actually going to pay the price of your sins for you. Yes, that was Jesus in our life story. It was Ward Cleaver in this episode of *Leave it to Beaver*. Wally and Beaver were trying to make money by selling the perfume. They sure couldn't afford to pay women to take if off their hands. That would go against the nature of their mission. The same can be said about our sins. We can't pay for them ourselves. There isn't an indulgence store down the street where we can purchase forgiveness. Someone had to reimburse us for our sins and that someone was and still is... Jesus. We need Jesus.

"We need Jesus," sounds like a simplistic statement. But really, what does, "We need Jesus," mean? How do we obtain Him? Where do we get Him? Why is Jesus necessary? Those are all great questions.

If you have already studied God's word and been baptized for the forgiveness of your sins, allow me to rejoice with the angels on your behalf. But I am sure some reading these devotionals may still be looking for God and if that is you, please reach out to someone who may be able to help you with a study and show you the answers for which you've been looking. And if you want, you can always just contact me through brianhumek.com/books.

**Dark Powers**

Episode 13 "Voodoo Magic" January 3, 1958
Written by Bill Manhoff
Bible Passage: Ephesians 6:10-13
Video Clip: 2:00-4:29

Prayer: *Dear God, Surround me with your protective power to keep me safe from all harm of Satan who is alive and well in our world. Please keep me safe from darkness of all sorts and keep it from my friends and family members too. Amen.*

Eddie Haskell is a rascal. He gets Wally and Beaver in trouble all the time. One of the first episodes in which this happens is "Voodoo Magic." The boys are going to the movies one Saturday and Wally blurts out they are going to watch *Voodoo Curse* at the Valencia Theater. June disagrees. They will go watch *Pinocchio* at the Globe Theater, no questions asked.

As Wally and Beaver walk Eddie over to the Valencia, Eddie convinces them to watch *Voodoo Curse* with him. As usually is the case when children disobey their parents, Wally and Beaver are found out and an appropriate punishment is doled out.

Beaver knows that if it wasn't for Eddie, he wouldn't have got into trouble. He'll get even with Eddie, but how? Well, Beaver creates a voodoo doll, writes "Eddie" on it and sticks pins into its stomach. When he finds out Eddie misses school the next day because he's sick, Beaver realizes the voodoo doll has worked.

Is such magic real? Does voodoo exist? The Bible doesn't address voodoo specifically, but it does talk about such things in a generic way in Ephesians 6 where it speaks of powers and principalities in this world. Evil is real in many different forms and it can damage you if you forsake God and begin believing in the evil powers more than Him.

Now, you may think pre-teens and teens could never be harmed by innocent games like Ouija (popular in the 1970s) or Dungeons and Dragons (popular in the 80s) or by having your kids attend a slumber party where kids chant "Bloody Mary" repeatedly and watch mirrors turn blood red. This is something I heard my friends talk about when I was young. You may think a fascination by your 12 or 13 year old daughter with the fictional character named Slenderman is innocent. If you do, there are many news stories that prove that untrue.

There are more avenues for today's youth to get entangled with the occult and its practices than in *Leave it to Beaver* days. Parents need to beware of what their kids are watching and reading and what consumes them most. Ephesians 6 isn't in the Bible just to take up space. God has those words in Ephesians 6 to help protect us, to warn us that Satan and his demons are alive and well and can play havoc in our lives and in the lives of those we love more than anything else in this world. Please be aware of the evil in your surroundings, but at the same time, do not use the evil in the world to hide from the world. Do not neglect the world and the people bound by evil. The best thing to do by far, is grounding yourself in God first, then entering the world to find others who need Him.

And by the way, Eddie Haskell was just fine. He was faking his original illness. Beaver didn't really harness the powers of darkness and evil to hurt Eddie, but I can't guarantee you he wouldn't do it if he could.

# BEAVER TIDBIT

**Eight Great Season One Eddie Haskell Moments**

Eddie Haskell is … well, let's make this poetic… a rascal. He sucks up. He tells stories that can't possibly be true. He gets others into trouble. He makes excuses when he can't do things right (like hit a baseball in "The Broken Window" or make a basket in "The Perfect Father.") Talk about a guy who shouldn't have a best friend like Wally Cleaver, the abovementioned personality traits should have had Wally running for the hills the first day he met Eddie. But Wally didn't and when asked various times over the six seasons of *Leave it to Beaver* why Eddie was his best friend, Wally typically replies, "Because Eddie says I'm his best friend."

There are many great Eddie Haskell moments over all six seasons of *Leave it to Beaver*, the following are the best from season one.

## 1. New Neighbors

The first appearance of Eddie Haskell was in "New Neighbors." After Beaver takes some flowers to the new next door neighbors, only the neighbor's wife is home at the time, and Eddie debuts his famous line, "Let's give him the old business." He and Wally give Beaver the "business" because Beaver kissed the new neighbor lady. "You see what happens in the movies all the time," says Eddie. He then makes a motion like a knife cutting his neck, implying death. Beaver has just experienced "the business" from Eddie Haskell for the first time ever.

## 2. Tenting Tonight

It is even possible to have a great Eddie Haskell moment without his being physically in the scene. In "Tenting Tonight," Eddie first tells the boys that their dad won't take them camping, that something will come up and he won't be able to take them to the woods. Well, unfortunately, Eddie was correct. But unlike Eddie's father who looked for excuses not to take Eddie on outings, Ward was not very happy to disappoint his boys. They wind up camping out in the back yard. It rains and Wally tells Beaver, "You know, Eddie Haskell says if you touch the inside of a tent while it's raining, it'll spring a leak." Beaver is not impressed, "Aw, that Eddie. He thinks he knows everything." Beaver then touches the inside of the top of the tent. It begins leaking. Wally surmises, after starting another leak himself, "That Eddie sure is a wise guy."

## 3. Voodoo Magic

Saturday is movie day for the Cleaver boys. They want to go to the Valencia Theater with Eddie to watch *Voodoo Curse* but June says no because Beaver is too young to see a horror movie. Wally is strictly prohibited by her to "take" Beaver to see *Voodoo Curse*. If the boys want to go see a movie, they will have to go to the Globe Theater to see *Pinocchio*. They bid Eddie goodbye at the Valencia as they are about to head on over to The Globe Theater. Eddie tries to convince Wally and Beaver to stay and watch *Voodoo Curse* with him. Wally explains that their mother said he couldn't take Beaver to see the movie. But Eddie does some explaining himself. "But she didn't say Beaver couldn't take you…" Convinced by Eddie they have their parents in a "gotcha" moment, the two Cleaver boys go watch *Voodoo Curse*. They also get appropriately punished when their parents discover their deception.

## 4. The Broken Window

Eddie comes to the rescue many times and this was one of the first times he gives Wally and Beaver deceitful advice that can possibly help them out of a jam. The jam in this case was a broken passenger side car window. Wally and Beaver were told not to play ball near the house and they figured one more swing of the bat couldn't hurt. It did. Now they had a broken window and they didn't know what to do. Eddie visits and gives them the simplest advice, "Roll down the window." If they just do that, the parents will eventually roll it up and see it's broken. He tells Wally and Beaver to be surprised when the broken window is discovered. In the end, the boys are honest, totally unlike that rascally Eddie Haskell.

## 5. New Doctor

In this episode, Wally is sick and stays home from school, a day in which he receives a magic set from his class, ice cream, the TV moved into his room and Beaver takes notice of the "goodies." The next day, Beaver says he too feels a little itch in his throat and begins to gurgle. He imitates all the symptoms Wally had the previous day. He gets into bed and stays there, waiting for the doctor to come by for a house call. About noon, Wally and Eddie arrive and Beaver figures out he chose to be sick on a half day. As the two friends are about to leave the room, Eddie looks back at Beaver, gives him the once over and knowing his scheme, gives some advice, "Boy, you better look sicker than that when the doctor gets here."

## 6. Cleaning Up Beaver

As with all appearances of Eddie Haskell at the Cleaver front door, one knows something smarmy is about to come out of his mouth. On this lovely afternoon, Eddie states he has come to get Wally because the two are going to the movies. A very dapper Eddie asks, "Do I look alright Mrs. Cleaver?" She assures him he looks fine and then smells an odor coming from his direction. "Smell quite nice too." Eddie informs her that the smell is his after shave lotion. "Why Eddie, do you shave?" He smugly replies, "No, but I like to smell like I do." His delivery of that line is comic genius.

## 7. Perfect Father

Eddie is allergic to mayonnaise so Mrs. Cleaver is reminded not to put any mayonnaise on Eddie's sandwich. The gang will devour their sandwiches when they take a break from playing basketball in Wally and Beaver's driveway. It's a big deal for Ward to have the kids playing at their house instead of at the Dennison's this afternoon. For some strange reason, Eddie can't make a shot. Even Tooey Brown can make one and he does so with his eyes closed. Eddie figures out the problem and suggests they measure the height of the backboard. Just as he thought, the backboard isn't regulation height. He convinces all the fellas to leave and go back over to the Dennison's house to play with a regulation height backboard. Mrs. Cleaver finishes making the sandwiches and puts mayonnaise on Eddie's sandwich because before encouraging the gang to go back to the Dennison's, he pushed Beaver. She makes sure Wally gives Eddie his sandwich. Oooh, that mean Mrs. Cleaver.

## 8. Boarding School -

Leave it to Eddie Haskell to stomp on a dream. When Wally decides he'd like to go to Bellport Military Academy instead of Mayfield High School, it doesn't take Eddie long before he's convinced Wally that the decision wasn't his at all. Eddie pipes up, "Yeah, when did your father get this idea?" You see, the previous year, Eddie's dad had begun hinting around about military school and he told his dad a thing or two. He even saw in a magazine that parents can't just get rid of you. Eddie with all his passion tells Wally, "Legally, they can't throw you out of the house until you're 21."

## Boasting

Episode 14 "Part Time Genius" January 10, 1958
Written by Connelly & Mosher; Story by Hendrik "Rik" Vollaerts
Bible Passage: Proverbs 27:2
Video Clip - :50 to 2:28

Prayer: *Dear God, Humble me. That is a very difficult request to make but in order to please you more I need to rid ungodly boasting from my life.*

Corny Cornelius likes to boast. Boy, does he love to boast! Ward Cleaver drops his co-worker off after a hard day at work but the man just won't leave the car. Instead, he sits there talking about his intelligent boys. His two boys are amazing and his younger son's teacher says there is no limit on how far he can go in life. Then, there is his daughter, that's where the real family traits shine through like a diamond. Ward may soon get physically ill if Corny doesn't cease his boasting.

Ward laments his kids aren't as smart as the Cornelius kids are. He finds out from Corny that the kids will be taking a huge test the next day and Beaver and Wally don't seem concerned at all about the next day's test. Wally informs Beaver after supper that the test is just an IQ test and for that type of test, there's no studying.

There's utter shock at the Cleaver house when the test results come back. Beaver receives the best score in the entire school, even better than the Cornelius kids. In fact, his score is the second highest in school history. Ward can't help but let Corny Cornelius know about how well Beaver did on the intelligence test. He does his own boasting. After all, what good is having a child if you can't boast about their accomplishments once in awhile?

Yes, maybe boasting about our kids is an innocent endeavor but in Proverbs 27:2, Solomon writes, "Let another praise you, and not your own mouth; a stranger, and not your own lips." There's something to be said for that because sometimes boasting can do harm.

When Ward arrived home after hearing Cornelius boast about his kids, the first thing that happened was he became disappointed with his own children. He envied the intelligence of another father's kids. Isn't envy a sin? Ward also brought some hostility into the house. His words after supper weren't merely for building up his children. God says don't do that. God says our words should encourage and build up people. Well, boasting is alive and well today and it still does some damage on occasion.

Don't believe boasting is alive and well, just check out Facebook. Psychologists have studied people and their Facebook usage and discovered that Facebook can make people sad or angry, depending on their personality and depending on how many people in their timelines are boasting about their absolutely wonderful and amazing lives. Whether the timeline boasts are about their kids, their job, their perfect spouses or just every other kind of blessing they've recently received in their life, this boasting causes some people to lament their own life. As there is with all social media, there's a tendency to post the fun, happy, good stuff about our lives and not the reality which is oftentimes not so chipper.

In Facebook life or real life, self-boasting can do damage. It can make you the talk of the water cooler at work and not the good kind of talk. Your boasting could make you a pest. It'd be great if we could just live amazing Christian lives, giving lives, unselfish lives that others want to talk about and maybe, just maybe, they will praise and boast about us themselves. That'd be a great thing to experience.

And do you remember what happens in the end of the episode "Part Time Genius?" Well, Beaver may just not be as smart as everyone thinks. Get on Netflix, MeTV or watch the DVD today.

## You're Invited!

Episode 15 "Party Invitation" January 17, 1958
Written by Mel Diamond and Ben Gershman
Bible Passage: 2 Timothy 4:7
Video Clip: 8:02-10:06

Prayer: *Dear God, If I fight the good fight, I know the outcome of life's trials will well be worth it. But getting through some days is simply difficult and almost too much to handle. Please help me finish the race, fight the fight and keep the faith. Amen.*

Beaver doesn't like girls. Of course, most little boys don't and now Linda Dennison, one of his classmates, has invited him to her birthday party. Beaver doesn't know it at the time, but he is the only boy invited to the party. He confirms this fact after calling some of his friends and asking them if they have been invited. None of his friends were invited for what turns out to be a delightful all-girl birthday party.

Beaver does everything he possibly can to make sure he doesn't go. But June and Ward insist he attend the party of a classmate, for not attending would be disrespectful. He reluctantly goes to the party. Talk about trials, James talks a lot about trials in his Bible book and this certainly counts as one for Beaver.

Ward drops Beaver off at the party and practically pushes him into the house and a gaggle of girls surrounds him, yelling his name and pulling him into the living room. The girls are excited to see Beaver and they play party games including Pin the Tail on the Donkey and Beaver even wins a drawing, the prize is a large doll. When a bit of boredom sets in, the girls come up with a great idea, "Let's play Post Office." Beaver's eyes grow big and he disappears into another part of the Dennison house.

Beaver has been steadfast and endured his trials but where's that eventual crown of life spoken about in James 1:12? Well, it's in Mr. Dennison's trophy room which is where he keeps all of his guns and heads of animals he has hunted on safari. Mr. Dennison wonders what had kept Beaver so long. He thought Beaver would've shown up in his room much sooner. Mr. Dennison assures Beaver that he too knows what it's like to be a rooster at an all-hen party.

Beaver endured and is now enjoying, what in his small world, is a crown of life. The gun collection is the greatest. There's a Sharps Carbine like Buffalo Bill used to kill buffalo and an occasional Indian. Beaver even gets to hold the guns and puts on a gun belt purported to belong to the infamous Billy the Kid.

What kind of trials do you endure? When have you been steadfast? The context of James seems to be speaking about life in general. That is the trial we all endure. Life isn't a bowl of cherries. Even those people we think are living inside a bowl of the tastiest cherries are not living there. Maybe cherries aren't so tasty to you and your preference would be a bowl of pink bubblegum ice cream. Well, no one's life is actually a bowl of pink bubblegum ice cream either. Life just isn't that way. It's difficult. Bad things happen. Yet, we endure and if we endure to the end, we are promised a crown of life.

When we're going through financial hard times, it's easy for us to look at someone driving a fancy car and say, "Man, I wish I could have a car like that" or "I wish I had their life." We don't know what kind of specific trials they may be going through. We may not even know if they're a Christian with the hope of a crown of life in the end. The same could be said about a healthy person when we ourselves are suffering with cancer or diabetes or some other ailment. We don't know the intimate lives of other people. Don't go wishing you were them, no matter how bad your life circumstances are.

Let us be happy that we, as Christians, have a crown of life waiting for us after we endure this big trial called life. Calling life a "trial" sounds pessimistic, but really, it's all in how you look at things. We can make a trial a challenge or we can make it a weight that holds us back and keeps us down. Have a good attitude and instead of calling life a trial, we'll just call it a challenge and we will succeed.

**Bullies**

Episode 16 "Lumpy Rutherford" January 24, 1958
Written by Joe Connelly and Bob Mosher
Bible Passage: 1 Samuel 17
Video Clip: 3:09-4:38

Prayer: *Dear God, Bullies are a part of life. Help me to deal with difficult people in a peaceful way that pleases you and fight battles only when they matter most. Amen.*

There is typically one thing all bullies have in common. They are bigger than the one they are bullying. Just look at Lumpy Rutherford in his *Leave it to Beaver* debut. He must outweigh Wally by fifty pounds. Beaver explains to their dad when asked how big this Lumpy is, that Lumpy is so big, "He's almost an adult." This bully named Lumpy is not allowing Wally and Beaver to walk down his street on their way home from school each day. The two Cleaver kids get their revenge, but that was probably something better left to God because their revenge goes awry and injures Lumpy's father Fred Rutherford.

We see in the Bible examples of bullying. I think about the Apostle Paul who bullied Christians, even to the point of death. The Pharisees were bullies too and they did it with legalism. They had lots and lots of laws and you couldn't break one of them or else. But those aren't examples that show a bigger person bullying a smaller person. No, that bullying example must be David and Goliath.

The battle between the Israelites and the Philistines seemed to be lost when Goliath from Gad showed his face and his really big body covered in armor. He taunted the Israelites, all nine feet nine inches of him. No one was brave enough to battle him one on one. That is until David shows up. However, that's when Goliath does some of his greatest taunting and trash talking. He said to David, "Am I a dog, that you come at me with sticks?" And the Philistine cursed David by his gods. "Come here," he said, "and I'll give your flesh to the birds and the wild animals!"

As is the case when anyone stands up to a bully, they fall, and they fall hard. Standing up to a bully does not always necessitate a fight with five smooth stones and a sling, but standing up to such people will typically accomplish good things in life. Two good things standing up to bullies will do for the world is that it will make you stronger and it will make the bully weaker.

There will possibly be times when we can't stand up physically or emotionally to bullies. Those times are tragic and are occurring more often each and every year.

Bullying in the 21st century is more multi-faceted than it was in the 1950s. Now, bullying can take place on social media, via emails, and websites. Because of this, there is no one answer to solve all forms of bullying, but I do like how Ward Cleaver speaks to Beaver about bullies of the old fashioned type. The best revenge or the best way to beat a bully says Ward in the end, is to not be like them. Don't act like a bully yourself and the one bullying will be the loser. They're doing bad and people, whether they are adults or kids who do bad, simply want someone else to do bad just like them.

God wants to help you with any bullies you encounter, whether these are co-workers, your boss, schoolmates or family members. He will provide you the patience or kindness needed to deal with them or if they are insufferable, God can provide you a way out of the situation, like a new job opportunity.

Be prepared to take God's help and you will defeat every bully that ever invades your space.

**First Job**

Episode 17   "The Paper Route"   January 31, 1958
Written by Fran Van Hartsveldt, Joe Connelly and Bob Mosher
Bible Passage: 1 Corinthians 9:24-25
Video Clip: 10:41-11:59

Prayer: *Dear God, Help me run the race of life to win the prize, not only the ultimate prize of heaven, but also those little tangible prizes that come into our lives here on earth. Amen.*

What was your first job? Did you sell candy door to door, mow lawns or shovel snow? What was the driving motivation behind your getting the job in the first place?

For Wally and Beaver, their first real job was delivering the Mayfield Courier, the local daily newspaper. Their motivation for getting a job was their desire for a new bicycle. They had shown their dad a picture of it and he confided that it looked like a pretty nice bike, which it should be for the price. The brothers admitted they had saved up some money to buy it and wanted to know if their dad could chip in some to help. They had raised $6.00 of the $52.00 price. That's when Ward suggested they get a job. He did so with one of his childhood stories of how he had done the same.

They promptly went down to see Old Man Merkel at the paper for a job and they convinced him to hire them. Over the next week, Wally and Beaver are gung ho about their new job. They persevere in making sure the route is taken care of responsibly. One day, they even traverse through a rainstorm to make sure the papers are delivered. The papers may have been soggy, but they were delivered. Then, one day, Beaver begins folding papers and intends to deliver them all by himself since Wally has a ballgame. They are determined to buy that bicycle. They have a final goal in mind.

How determined are you when it comes to your goals? Are you one that perseveres or do you easily give up? If you tend to give up, I can imagine your life has been quite difficult at times. If we persevere, it is almost always rewarded in some way or another. Sometimes that reward for persevering may only be the influence we have on others who see how we tackle certain obstacles in life. Our reward may be the inspiration we give them. There are areas of my own life where I continue to persevere despite obstacles, trying to attain a goal but have yet to see the fruit of my perseverance. I hope I at least am showing my son a good example and one day, he will see the big pay off. Is there anything in which you persevere and have yet to see the fruit? Can you explore this experience a bit deeper to see if you can find any hidden fruit of this experience? I bet you can find it.

Of even more importance than persevering when we are writing a book, trying to attain a certain job, or overcoming an illness, we can see perseverance in the way we walk with Christ to be the most important thing we can do in our life because one day we will all die and face judgment.

The reason I say it is so important to persevere in our walk with Christ is because of what happens when we become apathetic, when we cease to care. When we become Christians, we need to always be moving forward, persevering in our travels with Jesus. If we cease moving forward, learning, fellowshipping, trusting, loving, then we will eventually move backwards in our Christian walk. Rarely, if ever, does a Christian get to a certain point and just rests, no longer going forward or backward. We are living beings and we will either persevere and move forward, or we will go backward and be in danger of one day forsaking God.

Whether or not we are members of churches which help us move forward and persevere is an entirely different story. Seek out people and a church which will be a help, not a hindrance to your persevering spirit. We need all the help we can get so we can persevere. Beaver and Wally wind up getting their new bicycle. They persevered and won their prize, let us do the same.

# A Lack of Communication

Episode 18 "Child Care" February 7, 1958
Written by Joe Connelly and Bob Mosher
Bible Passage: Genesis 11:1-9
Video Clip: 8:30-11:02

Prayer: *Dear God, Help me always communicate clearly and with humility to those I interact with on a daily basis and I thank you for never cutting off the line of communication between You and me. Amen.*

There are many languages in this world I cannot understand. I think that's the same for most people who were born and raised in the United States. There are jokes around the world about our inability to speak other languages. Allow me to relate one to you now. What do you call someone who speaks two languages? Bilingual. What do you call someone who speaks three languages? Trilingual. What do you call someone who speaks one language? American.

Let us name some different languages in the world. There is Hungarian, German, Swahili, Mandarin Chinese, English, Serbian, Cherokee, baby talk, Java, C+, PHP and a wealth of so many others. Yes, I have included computer languages and baby talk on this list.

One wouldn't think a four year old would talk baby talk or speak about objects or places in words that aren't what they are. That could cause a big dose of miscommunication. That's exactly what happens when Wally and Beaver are charged with taking care of Puddin', the daughter of Ward and June's friends they are accompanying to a wedding. The boys are getting along mighty well in their first babysitting job ever until Puddin' keeps demanding to see Mary Jane. Is that a doll? Is it the name of her cat? The boys are getting a bit worried until their mom calls to check up on them. They relate Puddin's request to see Mary Jane and find out that Mary Jane is Puddin's term for the bathroom. Ohhhhhhhh.

When one person does not speak the language of another there is an absolute and unmistakable communication problem. That was the case with Puddin' and the boys. Why in the world would a four year old call the bathroom Mary Jane is beyond me, but this was a great example of a lack of communication, a speaking of another language that the boys could not understand, not in the least. But why do we have language barriers in the first place? We'll have to open our Bibles way back to Genesis to see how different languages came about.

I guess you can say, as with so many problems in the Bible, it began with pride. When the residents of Shinar (or Babylonia) wanted to build a tower, they said they could build one to the heavens, all the way up to God. Oh really? God didn't like this pride in their abilities. They gave no credit to God for anything and here they are now going to raise themselves to the level of God, at least physically, or so they thought. It was right then that God caused the people to speak different languages. Their talk sounded like babel, non-sense, hence, the tower they were building became known as the Tower of Babel.

No longer could the workers understand one another. They could not continue building the tower to the height they wanted. There were now many languages in the world when before this time, there had only been one. Communication would not be nearly as easy as it had been before. This is a dilemma we still face in our world today, especially with the balkanization of America and keeping people separate with their own languages instead of America being a melting pot like it used to be. This same problem has caused strife in Canada and in Quebec in particular.

The lesson to be learned is that God should be credited when we accomplish great feats. While we are wonderfully and beautifully made beings, we really are nothing without Him. Let us not be so prideful that we take credit for the good in our lives. We receive blessings and all blessings come from God.

One of those blessings to me is television, especially *Leave it to Beaver*. Trouble ensues after Puddin' gets to see "Mary Jane" but to find out exactly what kind of trouble, you'll have to watch this episode on DVD, MeTV or on Netflix. If you haven't yet seen this episode, I know you'll enjoy it.

## Showing Kindness

Episode 19 "The Bank Account" February 14, 1958
Written by Phil Leslie
Bible Verse: Ephesians 4:32 Bible Passage:
Video Clip: 8:29-10:19

Prayer: *Dear God, Kindness is a trait everyone has in one degree or another. I ask you today to grant me a bigger portion of kindness and that I show it to the world on a daily basis. Amen.*

Kindness presents itself many times throughout the *Leave it to Beaver* series. One of the most heartfelt and touching examples is seen in the episode "The Bank Account." Here, we see the boys save money in their piggy bank and after two months, they wind up with over $30.00. That's a lot of money for two boys in 1958.

The question is, "What to do with all that money?" Maybe they'll buy some sports equipment, a new catcher's mitt for Wally and a new fielder's glove for Beaver? The total of those two items will only come to about $14.00. Ward looks at their old baseball gloves and comments on how they only need a little sewing up. Even he has to do without sometimes. He's going hunting with Mr. Dennison on Saturday and he wishes he could have a new hunting jacket but he cannot afford one. So after a little prodding from their father, they decide to put the money in their school bank account and forgo spending any of it on new baseball gloves.

Before leaving for school, they stop by the hall closet to get their jackets. They pull out something that looks like it should be thrown away. They figure out it's their father's old hunting jacket. Wally comes up with an idea. They should buy him a new hunting jacket since he's always buying them stuff. Wow, this is unselfish kindness at its best. They don't deposit money in their accounts and even worse, at least to Ward, they each take additional money out of their accounts.

Ward did what many parents might do, he jumped to a conclusion. He jumped mighty high too. In the end, he needs some forgiveness from Beaver and Wally. After all, he thought he was now the father of two very selfish children who are underhanded, sneaky and irresponsible with their money.

God calls us all to kindness. Many times this is mentioned in His word. Are we as good as Wally and Beaver at showing kindness with our deeds and not just with our words? If we aren't, maybe we should think of the reasons why not. Maybe we should examine ourselves and make a better effort at kindness. Sometimes, we don't know exactly what God's will is for our lives, but when it's written down so plainly in text, we need to pay attention. God calls us to do a lot of things specifically, but one of the important ones is "be kind." In Romans 12:20, Paul writes we should even be kind to our enemies.

When we do exhibit kindness, don't expect something in return like gratitude or some monetary enumeration. I don't think our actions would be called kind if we only performed such acts for what we could get out of them. In the case of Wally and Beaver, it's fortunate they didn't expect anything good in return for this act of kindness, for all they received was a verbal scolding from their dad...until that moment when he saw the new hunting jacket.

My plan is to make someone that happy with an unexpected act of kindness. I hope you make it your plan too. The person who receives your act of kindness and your Heavenly Father will both be extremely pleased.

## Lonely

Episode 20 "Lonesome Beaver"   February 28, 1958
Written by Joe Connelly and Bob Mosher
Bible Passage: Gen 1:2 / 1:26
Video Clip: 4:29-7:28

Prayer: *Dear God, for those times I am lonely, thank you for always being there for me, whether I realize that fact in that moment, or if I realize it weeks, months or years later. Amen.*

Wally is leaving Beaver behind. He's growing up and going places where Beaver is not allowed to follow. In this particular instance, Wally and his friends are joining the local scout troop. Beaver tags along as they all go to register. But to Beaver's dismay, he is not allowed to join because he is three years too young. Wally tells the scoutmaster Beaver is a real good guy and that he'd make a great scout, but to no avail. Beaver then decides to walk home all by himself on a windy and stormy night.

It doesn't feel good to be left out of a group, even if it is a peripheral group such as Wally and his friends are to Beaver. But Beaver has been allowed to belong to that group on occasion, sometimes with caveats like having to earn more money to belong to a club or having to go out and earn money to buy a baseball uniform. But now, there will be no caveats, no exceptions to belonging. He's just not allowed to belong to this group now.

When have you felt like you did not belong? Oh my, I can go on about that for almost two hundred pages as I did in the book Purple Ducks. Buy it today to see a more in depth discussion on this subject of belonging or not belonging. But back to my original question, when was the last time you felt like you didn't belong? Were you fired from a job? Did friends or people you thought were your friends whisper in front of you? Did you get picked last in gym class for the dodgeball team? People can exclude you for the dumbest of reasons and in the most dumb of situations.

But why did Beaver feel so bad about being alone, being left out? It's pretty simple if you spend some time thinking about it. I don't know if I've been left out so often that I've dwelled on the topic a disproportionate amount of time or whether I just want to help others belong so much that I did research about the topic. Whatever the reason, I do know a thing or two about why we need to belong. You caught that word, right? We don't just want to belong. We "NEED" to belong.

The reason is found in the first chapter of Genesis in the story of creation. Read the entire chapter to fully grasp the idea but here are a couple verses to focus in on if you are short of time. In Genesis 1:2 we find the Spirit is hovering over the water. Then, later in Genesis 1:26 we see that God says, "Let us make man in our image." I understand not everyone reading this book is a Christian and will not automatically know that this is a mention of the Trinity, the concept that God is three persons but one entity. You have the Holy Spirit in verse 2 and have God and Jesus in verse 26.

We and everything else in this world were created in "community." It wasn't just the grandfatherly figure named God that waved a magic wand and said, "Let there be light… and camels and wombats and man and a helper for him, etc. etc. etc." The Holy Spirit and Jesus were right there with him. The figure we call God does not want us to be alone, because He wasn't alone when he created us. This is a concept that is more easily accepted with faith than it is to prove as a concrete fact. But think of God in three persons being similar to items we see in everyday life, for example, look at eggs, water and trees. With an egg, there is the egg white, the egg yolk and the egg shell. Then look at water when it's frozen, when it's melted and when it is turned into a gas. Or better yet, look at a tree which has roots, branches and leaves.

All a bit confusing? Well, maybe. But just remember that God created us to be with other people. Beaver didn't like being alone and neither do we. So if you love God and find yourself without a good church home, find one today. Need help finding one? Send a message via the contact info in the front of this book and we'll get you plugged in somewhere so you won't have to suffer being alone any longer.

# Clean

Episode 21  "Cleaning Up Beaver"  March 7, 1958
Written by Bill Manhoff
Bible Passage: Acts 2:36-2:41
Video Clip: 10:28-12:50

Prayer: *Dear God, Thank you for providing a way to have all my sins taken away so I can live in heaven where there will be no pain or sorrow, for eternity. Amen.*

It is sometimes difficult to get little boys to take a bath. They act like cats and run whenever the water is turned on. They actually, I guess it depends on what little boy it is, take pride in staying away from the bathtub. Sometimes little boys boast they've worn the same pair of socks for six days in a row. Ewwwww! Beaver went through this same stage and his problem with dirtiness happened to coincide with a time in Wally's life when he wanted to be clean in order to appeal more to the 8th grade girls.

If you've ever had a brother or a sister, you know there are a lot of things siblings can argue about. Some items on that list could include, who gets to go to the ballgame with dad, which sibling is their parent's favorite, who gets to play with a certain toy, what TV channel to watch, etc. But one wouldn't think that Wally and Beaver would argue about one of the two being too dirty and one of them being too clean, but that's exactly what they did. No matter how much any little boy enjoys being dirty, there always comes a time in life to have the dirt washed away.

If you're a member in a Church of Christ, it probably wasn't difficult for you to see where this devotional thought was going. Yes, be clean, step into the baptistery and be passive and let Jesus wash your sins totally away.

Just like Wally wanted Beaver to be clean, God wants the same for us. He knows this world is full of dirt and muck and grime and that it will get all over us, unless we hide in a cave all day like the hermits of olden days and spend our time praying and reading

God's word. Fortunately, that's not the way we live today, hidden away from the world.

God wants us to have our sins forgiven and for us to receive the Holy Spirit and go to heaven. God states specifically in His word, that these two things happen when we are baptized underneath water (Acts 2:38). It's amazing.

People like to argue about baptism, but there really is no reason to do so. More people every day come to realize that "being baptized" is a passive act, not some attempt at doing a good work, thus, saving ourselves. If you haven't already been baptized, study God's word, and seek out someone who will baptize you, not to show the world that you love God, but to receive the gift of forgiveness and the Holy Spirit.

When it comes to the act of baptism, the Bible is straight forward and doesn't seek out some sort of middle ground like Beaver and Wally agree to in "Cleaning Up Beaver." In this episode, Wally agrees to not be so very clean, and Beaver agrees to no longer be the mess he has been recently. As always happens at the end of each 30 minute episode, all ends well in Mayfield, USA.

## Helicopter Love

Episode 22 "The Perfect Father"   March 14, 1958
Written by Connelly & Mosher; Story by Fran Van Hartesveldt
Bible Passage: 1 Corinthians 13
Video Clip: 16:18-19:18

Prayer: *Dear God, Help me to be more trusting in the relationships you have blessed me with. If I truly have love for the people in my life, allow me to show it with trust.*

We always think about the love passage in 1 Corinthians 13 as only applying to spouses, but what about our kids? Don't our kids need to see us be patient, kind, not keeping track of every single thing they do wrong?  On top of that, I think our kids would like to see us be trusting, have hope and not be easily angered. So I think 1 Corinthians 13 also applies to parents in their relationship with their kids. I also believe that if we are going to exemplify those traits to our kids, we won't be parents who act like helicopters; you know what I mean… hovering parents.

As *Leave it to Beaver* fans watch the show either in reruns, DVDs or on Netflix, we rarely see the parents hover over Wally and the Beav. In fact, the exact opposite may be true. We may think Ward and June are just way too permissive, allowing their kids to stay outside on Saturdays for the entire day. How many of us let our little kids do that these days in our present society? It's a different world than was Beaver's in the 1950s.

Well, it seems like in "The Perfect Father," when the kids are spending all day outside, they are now doing it at the house of Willie Dennison, a friend who has a basketball goal and a father who takes them places. Ward, a typical father, gets a little jealous of his boy's new favorite place to hang out. He expresses his hope that as they spend more time at the Dennison's house, that they have not found a new, "home away from home." June exasperates matters when she says she hopes the boys haven't found a "father away from father." Oh my, talk about a mother piling onto a bad situation, that must have hurt.

The solution to Ward's problem is installing a basket with a backboard on their garage. He wants the kids to play at their house and that happens for a while until Eddie Haskell determines the new backboard is one foot too low and not the regulation height of ten feet. That afternoon, Ward makes the basket regulation height and the gang winds up back at the Cleaver house. That's when things get even worse. Ward goes out and tries to be one of the guys. He shows them some tips on how to shoot a perfect hook shot. The entire gang just wants to play basketball, not have someone's old man coach them on the finer points of the fancy hook shot. While Ward shows off his talent, hitting at one point, twelve shots in a row, the entire gang decides to leave and head back to Willie's house.

Later, Ward plays golf and runs into Willie's father, the object of his jealousy. He thanks him for being there to play basketball with the kids and Chuck Dennison laughs it off and tells Ward he didn't even know the kids were playing basketball at his house. But all the while, Ward had thought Mr. Dennison was right out there with them shooting hoops. Mr. Dennison says he learned a lesson with his two older boys and that was this, "The secret to getting closer to your kids is knowing when to stay away from them."

How many of us our hovering helicopter parents? While we need to protect our kids from some things, there are times when they simply need their distance (from us). They need to grow up and become independent. After all, we won't be here forever. "Trusting" is one of the things love is and we have to trust our kids eventually. This is something I struggle with mightily, but hope to overcome at some point in the future, hopefully before it's too late.

## The Holy Spirit

Episode 23   "Beaver and Poncho"   March 21, 1958
Written by Joe Connelly and Bob Mosher
Bible Passage: John 16: 7-16
Video Clip: 20:17-22:17

Prayer: *Dear God, Thank you for providing a comforter, a counselor, your Spirit, to be part of our lives. I thank you for the simple way we receive the spirit, in our baptism, so we can have a deposit on our residency in heaven. Amen.*

Imagine if Jesus told his Father in heaven that he wanted to stay on earth just a little bit longer so his disciples would better remember him. That would seem a little bit ridiculous. But then again, Jesus wasn't a little boy with a mind that had not yet matured. Jesus may not have ever had said such a thing, but that's what Beaver Cleaver did in today's episode, "Beaver and Poncho."

It all began with a trade. You remember trading stuff as a kid, don't you? In *Leave it to Beaver,* trades consist of exchanging items like an old slingshot for a frog or three pieces of candy for a handful of dead worms. Rarely would anyone trade a dog but… if the dog isn't yours, why not? That's what Larry Mondello traded to Beaver one rainy afternoon. But Beaver was told when he got home that he couldn't keep a lost dog. They would have to put an ad in the local newspaper. The ad Beaver wrote was a hodgepodge of words which could hardly be understood by the woman at the classifieds counter. "I'll rewrite it to make it clearer," she says. Beaver tells the absolute truth when he states, "Don't make it too clear. I want to keep the dog."

Finally, after a few days, a woman telephones the Cleavers and describes her lost dog perfectly. She will come by the next day to recover her dog, whose name, she tells them, is Poncho. When morning arrives, Beaver supposedly leaves the dog in his room as he goes to school, but actually takes the dog, a small Chihuahua with him. Beaver arrives home that afternoon and there is confusion in the Cleaver household. The dog is missing. Beaver then reveals that he took the dog with him to school. He wanted to spend more time with Poncho because he wanted the dog to remember him.

Imagine now, if Peter or John, right after the Last Supper had kidnapped Jesus, hiding him in a closet of that upper room, just so they could keep him a little longer, merely because they wanted Jesus to remember them. To tell the truth, that actually sounds like something Peter might do. I think if there was an IQ test given to the disciples; Peter might not even score as high as Beaver.

But Jesus said, do "this" in remembrance of me. He gave the disciples a memorial which would help them keep Him with them, at least in some small way. That's what the Lord's Supper is for Christians. But even more than the Lord's Supper, Jesus told the disciples that He was going to go away, but for them not to worry because He would send someone to comfort each of them. He would send a helper, the Holy Spirit. Repeatedly, Jesus calls the Holy Spirit with the personal pronoun, "He." The Holy Spirit is real. The Holy Spirit is active. The Holy Spirit is given to us as gift of God when we are baptized (Acts 2:38).

Praise God we have such a helper and that we don't have to hide Jesus in the closet or do anything else to have him remember us. He's with us still today and always will be. That is a comfort to know.

# BEAVER TIDBIT

**Leave it to Beaver Websites and Facebook Pages**
(listed alphabetically)

## Websites

### JerryMathers.com

Of course, if you love *Leave it to Beaver*, you must go visit Jerry Mather's website. You can find out a lot of information on Jerry in his own words. Visit the site regularly to find out what Jerry is up to. He lists some of his public appearances, the charities he's working with and he posts something new almost every month, and sometimes twice a month. Be sure while visiting the site that you click on his social media links. Jerry is very active on Facebook and has almost 40,000 people who like his page. Jerry also tweets, but most everything he posts on Twitter is also found on Facebook. So whether you tweet or use Facebook, you'll want to be connected to Jerry via his social media accounts.

### LeaveittoBeaver.org

Tim Schmitt is a dedicated *Leave it to Beaver* fan. He is the brains and creative power behind LeaveittoBeaver.org. There's an amazing amount of information to be found here that isn't easily found elsewhere. Some of it is unique to his site alone. One of the best points of interest found on the site is his email correspondence with actor Stanley Fafara, the actor who played Whitey Whitney and who battled substance abuse for many years. I have a few quotes from their email exchange in the Stanley Fafara biography in *Leave it to God,* but there is a treasure trove of interesting facts waiting to be discovered in their entire email exchange at Tim's website. There's a great FAQ section on the site as well, and one question asks, "Hey I want to buy X item. Do you sell it?" Tim's answer makes his site my favorite *Leave it to Beaver* fan website, "No, I don't sell anything." Bravo Tim! Check out his site today, but I'm guessing you already have.

## LITB.com

This site claims to be the "first *Leave it to Beaver* website." It was created by *Leave it to Beaver* fan Mark Smeby. There is a lot of good information on the site, but you have to muddle through quite a bit of advertising to find it. This is a very commercial website and is not updated as of October 2014. I found many links to pages not found (404 pages). Mark has also written a *Leave it to Beaver* Trivia book which you may find of interest. It is only available as an ebook and there's not a lot of information about it. Maybe he'll one day convert it into a Kindle book, let's hope so. One tidbit he includes in the site I found very interesting was his research on the comic book used in the episode, "Captain Jack." Remember, they found an ad for an 8-foot alligator and sent away for it. Mark provides a color copy of the original comic book which was published just the month prior to filming the episode.

## TonyDowSculpture.com

The name sort of gives the content of this website away. It is not a website dedicated to *Leave it to Beaver* or acting. However, his bio page does mention his years in Hollywood since acting and directing was his life for many years. So be prepared to step into Tony's artistic world. He is a very talented sculptor and he creates burlwood and bronze sculptures that have been seen around the world. He even had one of his pieces exhibited at the Louvre in Paris, France. Check out all of his work and purchase a piece or two for that special place in your home or office. And by the way, don't forget to click on his cityscapes, artifacts and assemblages pages. I overlooked them the first few times I visited Tony's site.

## Facebook Groups or Pages

There are many different Facebook groups and pages dedicated to *Leave it to Beaver*. The two I am including today are the best. I enjoy them and I know you will too and one of the reasons is because they aren't overly commercialized. Yes, they will post an occasional *Leave it to Beaver* book for sale, but that's about it. And yes, I hope they post this book. While I may be more active on one of these pages, I love them both equally. They each have high quality content and high quality members.

### Leave it to Beaver Fanville

With over 700 members, Leave it to Beaver Fanville is a very active page. The owner of this fan page is Paul and he has some story to tell of why he loves the show and why he keeps this page active with posts every single day. Often, Paul posts screenshots with closed captions so visitors can read the dialogue. A typical post will have 4-8 comments and 2-3 shares.

But again, I have to relate some of Paul's story as to why he started this Facebook page and why he loves the show so much. Better yet, let me share with you some of what he has to say:

*"The purpose of this fan page is to celebrate a show I love and watched while in the hospital with a rare (non-smoker) lung disease called Cryptogenic Organizing Pneumonia, a form of interstitial Lung Disease. I was on life support for 6 hours, intensive care for 24 days and in another rehab hospital for 23 days, a total of 47 days. I am still on a long road to recovery. While in the hospital the Beav and Wally brought such fond memories back, but also kept me smiling and happy. A true way to heal."*

Paul says it is important for him to post daily to Leave it to Beaver Fanville and I appreciate his hard work. The "About" section contains a list of rules that everyone follows and there is a good community of members who love the "simpler" times which Paul has spent his own money on via Facebook ads, trying to get more people to see and appreciate.

You must visit Leave it to Beaver Fanville today. I hope you become a fan so I can interact with you and find out all about your favorite episodes. You'll love the straight forward *Leave it to Beaver* trivia found here and even those hidden goodies Paul asks everyone to find in various *Leave it to Beaver* pics he posts. You'll have a good time in Fanville.

## The Leave it to Beaver Fan Club

With over 800 members, The Leave it to Beaver Fan Club group is extremely active. A typical post will have anywhere from 15-30 likes over a day or two and about 5-15 comments. There are a lot of friendly and helpful people here. The page was started by Mark Smeby, the founder of LITB.com, the first *Leave it to Beaver* website. Unlike a Facebook page, this is a group where everyone is free to post their own *Leave it to Beaver* memories or trivia in the timeline and so far, they haven't kicked me out for over posting, so I'd have to say this is a great group of people to hang around.

I have found that a lot of different people enjoy Leave it to Beaver and I learned that right here in this group. There are Christians, Atheists, Republicans and Democrats, cat lovers and dog lovers, Dallas Cowboy Fans and Philadelphia Eagle fans. Seriously, the people who love *Leave it to Beaver* are very diverse. I am proud to be part of this group.

If you're not already a group member, become one today. Just type the name of the group in your Facebook search box and you'll find it. Join it and take part in all the fun and memories. You'll be happy you did!

## Government Officials

Episode 24 "The State vs. Beaver" March 26, 1958
Written by Joe Connelly and Bob Mosher
Bible Passage: Romans 13:1-7
Video Clip: 9:40-12:11

Prayer: *Dear God, I find it hard to submit to authorities sometimes. I grumble about laws or other aspects of government. Please help me submit to the government while at the same time understanding that you are our only king. Amen.*

It's not fun to watch Beaver get into trouble. I think that's the reason why I never really liked his friend Gilbert. Whenever he hung around him, Beaver always got into trouble, but Larry Mondello also helped Beaver get into plenty of trouble too. However, there was something more sweet and innocent about Larry.

One of the first times in the series where Larry was responsible for Beaver's misfortune was when he talked Beaver into driving the new go kart he and his brother had built. He wasn't supposed to drive it on his own and Larry easily convinced Beaver he wasn't going to be alone, he'd be right there with him, so it must be okay for him to drive it. True to his word, Larry was right there next to him as he drove the go kart down the street.

Wait a minute. Kids can't drive go karts down city streets, well, at least not back in the late 1950s. They may do it today but I think rather than it being legal, a lot of people just turn the other way, preferring kids to drive a go kart down the street than running the streets as part of a gang or shoplifting at the local Dollar General. Anyway, back then, the police took such illegalities seriously. Beaver was stopped, not for speeding, but he was given a ticket for operating a motor vehicle without a license.

You too, may have been given a ticket for some sort of law you broke. Most likely, it was a speeding ticket or a ticket for turning right on red when that wasn't allowed. Those are two tickets I've endured. I wasn't happy about those tickets and I sure didn't want to pay them. I wanted to tell the judge that I'm a very good

Christian and that I write devotional books that everyone loves. I wanted to tell him I didn't need to pay the tickets because what I did wasn't really that bad after all.

But somehow I knew that it was right for them to ticket me and anyone else who broke a law. I'm not sure if I had really studied in depth the concept of how God instituted whatever government we have here in our city, state and country, but in my heart I knew the judge had the right to make me pay the ticket. I knew I'd also be in trouble if I didn't.

Even Jesus when he was sentenced to die told Pilate the only reason he had a right to sentence him to be crucified was because God gave him that power. In Romans 13, we find every reason necessary for us to pay our taxes, to stop at red lights and to obey every other law given to us by our local, state and federal governments. There needs to be order in this world and God always has known that laws help bring order and peace. And while we may not enjoy paying taxes, we need to do so because God gave us or instituted our governmental system. He says that government is only to be a terror to those doing bad, not those doing good.

If we do good, we have no need to be afraid of our government, even though I'm sure I and maybe some of you can come up with examples of governments who go rogue and do harm to innocent people. In the end, I think if that happens, God will do the punishing. It's not ours to seek revenge.

**Breaking Glass**

Episode 25 "The Broken Window" April 2, 1958
Written by Joe Connelly and Bob Mosher
Bible Passage: Proverbs 16:13
Video Clip: 12:59-15:05

Prayer: *Dear God, Please provide your guidance and help so the truth is told more often in my life whether this is in my daily discussions with friends, co-workers and family or in my daily prayers with You. Amen.*

Telling the truth is one of the more difficult things to do as a child, especially when doing so is a sure fire way of getting a whippin', grounded or both. A very familiar plotline in many classic television shows featuring kids is the broken window. "Who broke that window?" could usually be heard yelled over the airwaves of prime time television most every night.

In this case, Wally and the gang are playing ball in the street in front of their house. Wally pitches to Eddie and finally, Eddie gets some wood on the ball. He smashes it and before Larry Mondello can catch it, the ball sails over his head and right through a pane of the living room window.

The breaking of the window happens right in front of Ward as he pulls into the driveway. All of the boys run away but Wally and Beaver have nowhere to run. At supper that night, Ward says all is forgiven and forgotten, but never ever ever ever are they to play ball near the house again. Well, the next morning before going to the park to obey their father, with their parents out for the morning, Beaver has Wally throw him one pitch, just one, but Beaver smashes it into the garage, off the wall and right into the passenger window of the car.

When Eddie Haskell arrives, he offers a quick solution, "Roll down the car window and deal with the problem later." Wally and Beaver both feel uneasy about being so dishonest (because they really are good kids deep down inside, unlike that rascal Eddie Haskell). After thinking about it a while, they do roll down the window. The next day arrives and after an evening and a morning of pretending everything was okay, the boys do the best they can to discourage their father from taking the family for a drive in the country.  When Ward asks June to roll up her window, the boys plead with their dad to keep that from happening. To their surprise, the window was not broken. It was a miracle.

Well, it wasn't really a miracle. The previous night, Ward had opened the car door and closed it and heard the smashing sound of broken glass. He thought he had broken the window and then had it fixed. The boys confessed to what they had done and Ward felt good that his boys could tell the truth when in fact; they could've got away with a lie.

It must have been difficult for Wally and Beaver to tell the truth that day. It's sometimes difficult for us to tell the truth too. Isn't that the trickiest thing to do when we become Christians? Not that we have a truth serum injected into our veins at the time of our baptism into Christ, but we are to live a life pleasing to God and that should include telling the truth.

There can be no more getting an extra $10.00 bill back in our change at the store and keeping it. We are Christians. We must return that extra money and that's a form of honesty that can hurt sometimes, especially if you're short on money. We can't ask our kids to answer the phone and tell them to say we're not home. It doesn't matter who we are trying to avoid, you can't tell lies like that or have your kids lie for you. You're a Christian now and you must show a better example to those around you.

Now there may be a fine line between telling the truth and having a modicum of tact. Telling the absolute truth could get a husband in the dog house when his wife asks, "Does this dress make my butt look big?" However, tact could be classified as another thing altogether.

The truth is something that makes the King happy. In the Cleaver household, that's Ward Cleaver. In Christianity, the king is our Father, God, in Heaven. Please our King today. Start small if you have to, but your lips should be dripping with truth the longer and deeper your walk with Christ becomes.

## An All-Knowing Dad

Episode 26 "Train Trip" April 9, 1958
Written by Joe Connelly and Bob Mosher
Bible Passage: Jeremiah 23:24
Video Clip: 19:50-23:50

Prayer: *Dear God, You know everything about me and yet, I oftentimes act in ways I should not. Help me to remember your constant presence and to behave in ways that will have you smiling all day long. Amen.*

A thirteen year old and eight year old boy, Wally and Beaver respectively, should not be allowed to buy their train tickets back home from Aunt Martha's all by themselves. Aunt Martha should've known better. Oh yeah, as Ward stresses many times during the first season of *Leave it to Beaver*, "Aunt Martha has no kids of her own." I guess that's her excuse for her not knowing that kids their age are not always the most responsible of people.

Their train back home was 45 minutes late leaving the station and what are two boys going to do in a train station to bide their time? Well, first, they're going to buy comic books and then they'll buy candy. Finally, they'll buy their train tickets and they then won't have enough money to buy tickets all the way back to Mayfield. That's trouble, especially when Beaver says he's scared and doesn't know what they will do when the conductor comes to check their tickets. Wally assures him that, "They only do that in the movies." When the conductor begins walking down their aisle calling out, "Tickets. Tickets. Get your tickets ready," that's when the boys slink in their seats hoping to be bypassed by the conductor.

The boys show the conductor their tickets, but those tickets were for the previous town. They make up a wild story about their dad falling out of an airplane and other misadventures and that's why they couldn't afford tickets to Mayfield. Unknown to the boys, Ward's friend George Haskell is sitting two rows back. He relates the entire happening to Ward the next day. Up in their room that night, Ward reassures Wally and Beaver that he'll be just fine after that terrible fall from the airplane. He also wants to make sure they take care of the situation with the conductor and pay him back for his covering their fare. In return, they assure their dad they will.

The boys are utterly amazed at how their father knew about what they had done. Wally surmises, "Sometimes your dad knows things you know there's no way he could ever know." Father's do seem a bit all knowing sometimes, especially when we do something bad. It's a little bit better with our Heavenly Father. He knows all the bad we do, but he also knows all the good. Not only that, he knows every time we're sad, lonely, when we lack self-confidence, when we're in need financially, spiritually and physically. Oh my, our Heavenly Father knows every little and big thing about us. He knows the number of hairs on our head. In some cases, he doesn't have to count very high, but he knows each hair.

I guess you could just say it like this, "God is very smart." Others would say he is, "all-knowing." While theologians or Christians who've attended church for years would expound on that and say, "God is omniscient."

God isn't just a Ward Cleaver who knows about things we do when someone calls him on the telephone who witnessed a particular event. God knows us intimately and wants us to have an abundant life. The amazing thing is, God loves us despite knowing everything about us. I think that's cool, don't you? Despite all our faults, He loves us still.

## Manipulation

Episode 27 "My Brother's Girl" April 16, 1958
Written by Joe Connelly and Bob Mosher; Story by Bill Manhoff
Bible Passage: Judges 16:1-22
Video Clip: 15:57-18:52

Prayer: *Dear God, You have made all people in your image. Help me to show the respect I have for you to all the people you allow to enter my life each day. Amen.*

Females reading this devotional, please do not be offended. I'm not making a blanket statement, but in reality, some women or girls use boys and men to get something they desperately want, which could be different things for different females. I know none of the female readers of this book have ever done such an outrageous thing, but it does happen on rare occasions.

When I was in fifth grade, a girl named Andrea pretended to like me. She did so just to have me share my peanut M&Ms with her. When they were gone, she actually told me she didn't like me and was just using me for my M&Ms. At least she was honest. Well, the same thing happened to Beaver Cleaver. He became caught up in the sticky web of deceit which was Mary Ellen Rogers.

If you're as big a fan of *Leave it to Beaver* as I am, you know exactly who Mary Ellen Rogers is and how important she eventually became to Wally. In fact, in *The New Leave it to Beaver* series which debuted in 1983, Mary Ellen and Wally are husband and wife. Well, it all began in the 27th episode of *Leave it to Beaver,* "My Brother's Girl."

There's an upcoming dance and Wally is going to go with the "guys" and not take a date. However, Mary Ellen has her eyes set on taking Wally and even June knows Wally will wind up going with her. Ward asks how she knows. Oh, silly Ward, huh? How it all occurs is Mary Ellen befriends Beaver at lunchtime at school. She then invites Beaver to come over to her house to play with her father's trains. She does this until Beaver is hooked. Then, when he wants to come over the next time, she says her parents are mad she has a boy over by himself, but if Beaver would bring someone, say, his older brother, that would be okay. Beaver ropes Wally into coming and they get to play with the trains.

While there with Wally, Mary Ellen constantly tries to brush off the Beav. It doesn't take him long to see he's been used to get Wally there. She doesn't care to have him around at all. Poor Beaver, he's fallen prey to the wily trap of a woman. But he's not alone. Some of the best men in the world have fallen into such traps. One such man was a strong man named Samson. They've even made movies about this guy and the woman who used him.

Delilah used her powers to seduce and deceive Samson. She didn't actually use him to get something special, like to get him to go to a dance, or to take her out to an expensive restaurant or to get a diamond ring. She used her beauty to get something even more important from Samson, the secret to his super human strength. Once she got that secret from him, his hair was cut and he was rendered powerless. She no longer needed him.

Men and women both have the power to use someone of the opposite sex for ungodly objectives. Sometimes that objective is sex. If you are single and are looking for love, that is laudable and something God wants you to have. But don't go so far that you end up using a person you love to fulfill an urge or a need you think needs to be satisfied. Live a godly life if you're a Christian. There are other ways to use people too. There's always a temptation to step over people, use them and then kick them out of the way when you are finished with them. Climbers of the corporate ladder, if they look down, can sometimes see a lot of people in a trash heap at the bottom of their ladder. We have become a society where we love things and use people and that's totally backwards from how it once was.

Remember, the next time you are tempted to use someone to either get your own way, move further along in your career or to satisfy a need, that the someone you may use, was created the same way you were… in the image of God.

**Look at Me!**

Episode 28 "Next Door Indians" April 23, 1958
Written by Connelly & Mosher; Story by Robert Paul Smith
Bible Passage: Matthew 6:5-6
Video Clip: 2:26-4:59

Prayer: *Dear God, Having the attention of others is important but please help me garner the attention of others only in ways that are pleasing to you. Amen.*

Eddie Haskell tells all sorts or stories to make him a big shot to the guys. Beaver sees this and imitates Eddie. Beaver pipes up that there was once an Indian battle that took place in the empty lot right across from their house. Beaver makes his lie believable because he bets Eddie $1.50 if he can prove it isn't true. The next day, the gang comes over with shovels and rakes, but not before Wally and Beaver bury some artifacts such as an arrowhead and an arrow, albeit, one made in Japan.

Eddie, always the doubter, when he sees the arrow, reads some printing on the shaft, "J-A-P-A-N." He looks at Wally and says, "I've never heard of no Japanese Indians. You guys buried this stuff here." Eddie was right. It was all just a ruse to get Beaver some attention. Not that attention is bad, but sometimes the way we get it can be.

God knows we all need it. We crave it. Attention is what makes the world pleasant at times. We want to know that people respect us and care about what we say. This is especially true in our marriage relationships, work relationships and even in church. Think about church for a moment. There are so many people who have left congregations, and sometimes church in general, because people ignored what they said or felt. Legend even has it that Mohammed went to the Christians and Jews to talk about his own new religious beliefs and was shunned, and then he began his own religion.

In Luke 18:9-14, we see an example of how people praying can beg for attention. A Pharisee prayed out loud, wanting everyone to see him, big booming voice, and not only that, because he was so loud and attracting attention to himself, he thought he was better than the publican who was next to him praying. That man prayed so much more quietly and with more humility. He didn't think himself better than the Pharisee.

Jesus even tells us to go into our closets to pray, not standing on a street corner making sure everyone can see us or hear us. In a church context there are people we await to hear pray because their prayers are beautiful and flowing with love and praise that can be very poetic. There are others who pray long prayers that seem to drone on forever simply because they crave the attention they get while standing in front of the people in the pews, or maybe not, but that is how it may seem to some people.

There are other ways to attract attention in church, complaining to the elders, complaining to the members, complaining to anyone who listens. That attracts a lot of attention and if you find sympathetic ears, you can be part of a group who demands things are done differently in your church. One can't get much more attention than that. And for people who complain a lot, that often entails made up stories, at least a few.

Attention getters can be found in schools, workplaces, the family supper table, basically anywhere. Those starving for attention are not the most fun people to be around. Do something good to grab attention. Don't make up stories like Beaver did because eventually, people will tire of you and your story telling. Eventually, even Eddie's friends throughout the run of *Leave it to Beaver* fail to take Eddie seriously and let his words go in one of their ears and out the other. And it all began in this episode of *Leave it to Beaver*.

## Let's Go Camping

Episode 29 "Tenting Tonight" April 30, 1958
Written by Connelly and Mosher; Story by Fred Shevin
Bible Passage: 2 Corinthians 4:8-9
Video Clip: 15;27-16:52

Prayer: *Dear God, When difficult times come my way, I need your help so I can make the best out of those times and to react in a Christian manner for all to see. Amen.*

What happens when you are gearing up for a great weekend and your plans fall through? Some people may pout, others may mope around the house, others may snap at family members because they simply didn't get their way. I'm not talking about only kids here, but adults too. Because we live in a fallen world, we oftentimes don't handle disappointment well. Remember though, that our reactions often say more about us than our actions.

I admit it was quite surprising to watch an episode of *Leave it to Beaver* in which Ward promises the boys a weekend of fun camping, exploring, and fishing up at Friends Lake and at the last moment, he has to cancel. Ward Cleaver always kept his word, right? What made things worse for Wally and Beaver is that know-it-all Eddie Haskell said from the start they weren't going to go. He knew that somehow, some way, their dad would cancel the trip, most likely because he had to work that Saturday.

Well, come Friday, that's exactly what happened. The boys then did something my Aunt Ellene always told me she did, that was when God gives you lemons, make lemonade. They decided to camp outside in the back yard on their own. They made a big pitcher of lemonade out of the lemons of not going to Friends Lake. I think that's exactly what the Apostle Paul did his entire life; he must have drunk a bunch of that lemonade too.

The book of 2nd Corinthians has some great examples and encouraging words from Paul about disappointment and trials of all sorts. He speaks about all of his trials in 2 Corinthians 11:23-35. The list is exhaustive and I wonder how any mortal man could endure all those trials. However, Paul was only a mortal, just like us, but he lived life with an immortal type of faith in God. Early in the book, he speaks about the trials we endure as ways to comfort others. That's a great attitude to take regarding our never ending travails. Finally, he speaks of being "hard pressed on every side, but not crushed…struck down, but not destroyed."

We Christians have a great ability to forget that we too can have what appears to be an immortal faith in God. You see, God created you and me in His image. That is the same way God created Paul and all other Apostles. We are all mere humans with the same abilities to have faith, to endure and to make the best out of bad situations. When we react positively to bad situations like Paul or as Wally and Beaver did, we show the world where our faith lies, where our allegiances lay; we show our good character when we drink a lot of lemonade instead of chewing on bitter pieces of lemon.

Make a commitment today to be a person of character who can react positively to negative situations. The people in your world will be impressed and notice you. They may even imitate you and help create a positive environment for everyone. Most of all, God will be happy you're drinking the lemonade of life.

**Fruit**

Episode 30  "Music Lesson"  May 7, 1958
Written by Connelly and Mosher; Story by Jean Patrick
Bible Passage: Galatians 5:22-26
Video Clip: 16:25-17:50

Prayer: *Dear God, I want to walk closer to you and every day show more fruit of the Spirit in my life. Please help me exhibit the fruit of a growing Christian.*

Beaver is feeling bad today because his brother Wally has just made the baseball team and his parents are gushing over his accomplishment. Beaver doesn't have anything with which to make his parents proud but he soon sets out to change that. He decides to go out for the school band and chooses the clarinet as the instrument on which he will excel. After his first few lessons, Beaver demonstrates to his family what he has learned. They cringe as he plays, but they do recognize the tune as "America."

Beaver continues with his lessons and on the big day for band tryouts, Beaver is politely told he cannot be in the band and should practice more so maybe he'll be able to join the following year. But at this time, he'll have to return the clarinet. Beaver practically begs to keep the clarinet for a bit longer and the teacher allows him to do so. A week later, Beaver gives another recital for his family. He plays the exact number of notes he did previously. While his parents cringe once more, upstairs, Wally gives him the third degree, wondering when he got kicked out of band class.

The way this all works is that when you stop practicing your clarinet, you'll not progress any further in your clarinet playing skills. Pretty simple, isn't it? Eventually, you'll regress and at some point in the future, you will not be able to play a single note. One could make the case that the Fruit of the Spirit is similar because each of those traits will increase the more often you "play" them or "use" them in your life. If you are indeed living by the Spirit, your life will be full of the Fruit of the Spirit. This fruit consists of the following: love, joy, peace, forbearance, kindness, goodness, faithfulness, gentleness and self-control.

When you're baptized, the Holy Spirit comes to live inside you. This is a mighty act and because of that, you are called to have the abovementioned traits. You will be more loving, have more joy, seek peace more often, bear with those who annoy you, be kind more and more, exhibit goodness and faithfulness and think of others before yourself and in all aspects of your life, have self-control, whether that may be in how much food you eat or how many shoes you buy or in your sexual behavior. This is what the fruit of the spirit in a believer's life looks like.

When we read about the fruit of the Spirit, the key verse is found in Galatians 5 verse 25. It reads, "Since we live by the Spirit, let us keep in step with the Spirit." God isn't telling us to run with the Spirit. He's not telling us to stand still with the Spirit. He only wants us to keep moving with the Spirit. He uses the words, "keep in step." The words absolutely illustrate forward movement. He expects us to show more fruit the longer we are Christians. That happens naturally in some Christians' lives. For others, it may take a lot of diligent prayer and Bible study and time spent with other Christians in order to keep going forward. We are all different and we all "keep in step" with the Spirit in different ways and at different rates.

The best thing any of us can do if we really care about keeping in step with the Spirit is to take a spiritual inventory every once in a while. Someone like me, I may have to take that inventory weekly. I need to ask myself how I'm doing, maybe even rate myself on my self-control and kindness and patience. Seriously, if we don't gauge how well we are doing, we may neglect going forward, something God would be sad to see happen in our lives.

## Crying Wolf

Episode 31 "New Doctor" May 14, 1958
Written by Joe Connelly and Bob Mosher
Bible Passage: Jeremiah 20:7-10
Video Clip: 11:30-12:29

Prayer: *Dear God, I look for your guidance in areas of my life where I feel like complaining and telling the world how bad things are in my existence. There will be extremely bad times but help me understand when I should speak, and when I should stay silent and simply listen to you. Amen.*

One wouldn't think that Beaver Cleaver and the prophet Jeremiah would have anything in common. Do I have secret knowledge that Jeremiah was an adorable little kid at times and annoying at other times? No, that wouldn't take secret knowledge, that describes all of us. Well, we'll figure it out by examining a bit closer, the episode titled, "New Doctor."

The day begins with Wally gargling water in their bathroom. He admits to Beaver that his throat hurts a bit. When June goes to their room to tell them breakfast is ready, Beaver lets her know Wally has been gargling and she immediately thinks Wally may be sick. She checks and he has a fever and is forced to stay home from school, missing a scheduled baseball game that afternoon. Wally isn't happy.

As the day progresses, a doctor visits the house and lets Wally and his mom know he'll be alright if he stays in bed. He should be able to go back to school the next day. Later, Eddie and Tooey come over and give Wally a gift from the class they decided to give him after they heard he was sick in bed. His dad brings home ice cream. Later, his dad brings the TV into his room. Lots of cool things happened when Wally was sick. That's not left unnoticed by Beaver.

It's not too hard to imagine that the next morning Beaver is gargling and complaining of a sore throat. He wants to get some of that "loot" Wally received. So Beaver does what some little boys will do, craving attention, he pretends to be sick. It is not until the doctor, not their regular doctor, but a new one, shows up that afternoon that Beaver realizes he is the subject of an Aesop fable.

His biggest concern up to this moment has been whether or not the new doctor was a "pill" doctor or a "needle" doctor. But now, after his check up, the doctor gives him a lecture good enough to be from a father. He tells Beaver that he is just fine. Beaver admits he's been fine all day. Well, Beaver has just admitted he's the boy who cried wolf. He's said something is bad when it wasn't. The doctor tells him there are a lot of sick people in the world who need a doctor and if all little boys did as he did, the people who are actually sick would not be able to see a doctor. What he did was not good. Whether or not he tells his parents is up to him. Beaver feels the guilt of his actions and eventually tells his parents.

Well, where's the comparison with the prophet Jeremiah? In the book of Jeremiah, the prophet repeatedly tells the people of Jerusalem that they will be punished for the bad they have done. He says this over and over again, but to no avail. The doom and violence he preaches doesn't come, at least not through the first 40+ chapters of the book bearing his name. In Jeremiah 20:10 the people are whispering against Jeremiah that he is Mr. Terror on Every Side. He's always predicting doom, but it never comes. While Jeremiah is prophesying the truth, the people in his time are thinking he's crying wolf.

We too can cry wolf without actually lying. What about our financial situations? We may tell others how bad things are in our lives. As a domestic missionary (church planter) I did this often via our newsletters. I did it so often when I thought things were really bad, that when things grew worse, the people to whom we sent our newsletters either glossed over our pleas for funds or simply deleted our newsletters without reading them.

The same could be said for health problems, other prayer needs, our children's behavior problems, etc. We may rail about them, lament about them and ask people for help but really the problems we're experiencing are minor compared to what they may become one day. People may think our problems are little and say we're crying wolf, even though we think our problems are really bad.

I think we can maybe wait to CALL IN the cavalry (our friends and family) to help with our problems if we more often would CALL ON Calvary (Christ) to help us with our problems. We sure wouldn't want to be accused of "crying wolf," now, would we?

# BEAVER TIDBIT

## The Viet Cong Didn't Kill Jerry Mathers, but Diabetes Almost Did

During the Viet Nam War, Jerry Mathers was rumored to have been killed by Viet Cong troops. He was in the Air Force, but never was stationed outside American soil. Nevertheless, somehow, a rumor was started that he had been killed. That rumor really took off after actress Shelly Winters, an outspoken opponent of the war, announced this tragic happening on the Tonight Show with Johnny Carson. Even Tony Dow believed this terrible news and sent flowers and his condolences to his parents' home. Needless to say, the rumor was false.

Over 20 years later, after the end of *The New Leave it to Beaver*, Jerry Mathers wasn't seeing much action on the set, on the tennis courts, in the workout room or anywhere for that matter. The worse thing he did post-*New Leave it to Beaver* was buying a catering business, but one could argue that continually eating food from the business was actually the worst thing he did. He gained 50 pounds and about 8 -10 inches around his waist. [15]

It wasn't until 1997 when a friend, a doctor who often saw Jerry at family functions, tried convincing him that he needed to visit the doctor and have his blood sugar checked. After putting off the doctor visit for quite a while, his friend insisted he get a physical and offered him a free one for Christmas. He had his blood work done and went back a few days later for the results. "My blood sugars were running around 540 mg/dl all of the time, and my

---

[15]　Jerry Mathers, interviewed by MeTV Monitor, January 28, 2014, MeTVnetwork.com.

---

blood pressure was running around 160 over 130 mmHG."[16] His doctor asked Jerry, "How'd you like to see your kids graduate from high school and go to college, get married, see your grandchildren?" He of course answered in the affirmative and she told him he'd be dead in two to three years if he didn't get his diabetes under control. [17]

Through help from a Jenny Craig weight loss program, Jerry was able to control his diabetes. He is now, no longer diabetic. His condition is considered pre-diabetic.

While Jerry still acts when the right part comes along, the one thing Jerry does on a regular basis is raise awareness about type-2 diabetes. He speaks many times a year about his past struggle with the disease and his continued fight against it. As he says in many interviews, "It's sort of like fishing. I go, I talk about *Leave it to Beaver*. I talk about working with Bob Hope, Alfred Hitchcock, Frank Sinatra and at the end, maybe the last 15 minutes, I start talking about my life now, about diabetes, and people don't really realize that they're learning a lot of propaganda about how to help themselves." [18]

Within 11 months of joining Jenny Craig, Jerry was able to lose enough weight to get his diabetes under control and to keep it under control while at the same time, saying goodbye to his diabetes medication. [19] Jerry has a passion for helping people and everywhere he goes, with each interview he gives, people are told the good news that diabetes can be defeated and many times, it can be done without the help of a pill or insulin. People only have to eat sensibly and keep excess weight off. While it may not be

---

[16] Daniel Checroci, "Jerry Mathers Leaves It to Weight Loss to Control His Diabetes," diabeteshealth.com, August 1, 1999, accessed September 29, 2014, http://diabeteshealth.com/read/1999/08/01/1609/jerry-mathers-leaves-it-to-weight-loss-to-control-his-diabetes/.

[17] Jerry Mathers, interviewed by MeTV Monitor.

[18] Jerry Mathers, interviewed by Ken Boxer, February 13, 2014, Ken Boxer Live.

[19] "Child Star Jerry Mathers," *Palo Verde Valley Times*, June 26, 1998.

pleasurable giving up foods we love to snack on, I think Jerry Mathers would say, "Consider the alternative."

While Jerry is a huge supporter and worker for diabetes awareness, one look at Jerry's blog (find it at **http://jerrymathers.com**) will show you numerous charitable organizations he supports or has supported over the years through speaking or volunteer work. They include: the L.A. Sheriff's Youth Foundation, the Neuropathy Action Foundation, the American Diabetes Association, the Special Olympics, AIDS Walk Orange County, Partners in Care Foundation, March of Dimes, and Easter Seals among many other worthy causes. [20]

In the final moments of his amazing interview with Gary Rutowski, he was asked how and for what he would like to be remembered. Jerry spoke eloquently about how fortunate he has been in his life and how he tries to give back to others as much as he can. He spoke about wanting to raise awareness about diabetes, psoriasis and aging and being remembered for helping with these causes that are dear to his heart. He does as much speaking as he can on the subjects and despite knowing his limitations, wishes he could do more. He also added with a chuckle that of course he'd be remembered for his role in *Leave it to Beaver*.[21]

---

[20] "Former Television Co-Star Beaver Cleaver of 'Leave it to Beaver'," KeySpeakers.com,accessedSeptember29,
2014, http://www.keyspeakers.com/bio.php?2015-jerry-mathers.

[21] Jerry Mathers interviewed by Gary Rutowski.

**Comfort**

Episode 32 "Beaver's Old Friend" May 21, 1958
Written by Dick Conway, Roland MacClane, Connelly and Mosher
Bible Passage: 2 Corinthians 1:3-7
Video Clip: 23:52-24:53

Prayer: *Dear God, You comfort me when I am hurt, not only once in a while, but all the time. Please bring people into my life who hurt so I can share with them the comfort you also provide me. Amen.*

Spring cleaning can help rid a home of a lot of junk. This must be the season garbage men dread the most. I personally have seen in spring trash piles on the streets around our home, in addition to tons of boxes filled with junk, everything from dirty rubber picnic tables to soiled carpets, disabled window AC units to a beat up roping dummy (we still have that piece of western Americana in our backyard). The Cleavers in "Beaver's Old Friend," are throwing away boxes of papers, an old shot-put, a tire cover from Ward's old roadster, half used cans of turpentine and Beaver's old stuffed Teddy Bear Billy.

His dad and Wally discard the stuffed animal as nonsense and something Beaver is too old to play with. He throws the bear, his friend, given to him by Aunt Martha when he was sick in bed with the measles, in the trash and waits for his dad and brother to leave before retrieving it. Then some friends come by and begin teasing Beaver for playing with a stuffed bear. Again, Beaver throws Billy in the trash. Beaver goes to play with his friends and while he is gone, the trash truck has come and hauled Billy away.

Beaver goes on a frightful search and finally finds Billy and brings him back home. Wally winds up understanding how much Billy means to Beaver. He suggests dousing the bear in perfume to get rid of the turpentine smell. The next morning at home, after attending worship and while the boys are still at Sunday school, Ward and June decide to clean up the boys' room. To their surprise, they find it spotless but reeking of perfume. They find the beat up bear. June says she's going to clean up the bear and make it good as new for Beaver.

After all the work June has gone through, Beaver thanks her but then, in what seems like an instant, wants to emulate the concept of comfort found in 2 Corinthians 1:3-7.  He suggests to his mom that when he had been sick in bed with the measles, Billy made him feel better. In other words, Billy had given him comfort when he was sick. He then tells his mom, using the logic of comfort, that he wants to give their neighbor boy Bengie the bear because he was sick in bed and that maybe Billy would now be able to make Bengie feel better and when he gets better, maybe Bengie could give Billy to someone else who is sick. The bear could go viral...I guess in more ways than one.

Beaver really has an understanding that Paul tries to get us to comprehend in 2nd Corinthians. We go through troubles sometimes and we might not understand why, but after our troubles, and often, because of them, we then can help someone else when they are experiencing the same problems in their own life. It is so easy for us to become consumed by self and not give thoughts to others. But God wants us all to help others and what a waste it is if we see someone who is going through the same problem we've experienced and decide not to help them make it to the other side of their troubled waters.

Let us offer others at least as much comfort as Beaver Cleaver offered his little neighbor Bengie. Whether we offer a stuffed bear or a listening ear, God will be pleased.

**Yes**

Episode 33 "Wally's Job" May 28, 1958
Written by Joe Connelly and Bob Mosher
Bible Passage: Matthew 5:37
Video Clip: 5:56-8:18

Prayer: *Dear God, Your word is filled with unconditional promises,
you've kept them all. I pray you will help me be as good at keeping my
word, at saying "yes" and doing exactly what I have told others I'd do.
Amen.*

If someone were to offer me $8.20 to paint two trash cans, I
would do it. I don't think that's an unreasonable salary seeing that it
would only take a few minutes. I'm not below manual labor, in fact,
I love it sometimes. In this episode Wally is offered $1.00 to paint
two garbage cans. In today's money, that would equal $8.20. Not
bad for a kid in 1958. Wally gladly accepts the job.

But when Eddie Haskell hears about this job, he almost cries out
that Ward is using Wally as slave labor. Eddie elaborates, "He'd
have to pay a stranger $3.00, why should he take advantage of you
just because you're unlucky enough to be a member of the family?"
That's when Wally gets nonchalant about doing the job. He puts it
off and then tells his dad he wants more money. He acts as if he's a
star football player holding out during training camp. Wally is not
an all-star garbage can painter and Ward tells him he should paint
them for the agreed upon price. Beaver takes all this in and sees an
opportunity to get the money guaranteed for Wally. His dad,
getting more upset with each passing day, passes the job along to
Beaver.

That causes a fight between the boys when Wally comes home
from school one day and sees Beaver painting the cans. Ward tells
him he promised and he needed to keep his word. Ward then
decides to give each boy 50 cents to paint one can each. Wally
accepts this and there's a spirit of forgiveness in the garage as they
paint. In the end, neither Beaver nor Wally paint the cans. Find the

episode on DVD or Netflix to see who does. Needless to say, the point is Wally should've kept his word.

How many times do you say you'll do something and an unexpected event happens and the deed or act you were going to do, doesn't occur? How many times have you promised to take your kids somewhere and, again, something just comes up at the last minute? What about at church? Have you told a deacon or minister you'll do the Lord's Supper talk or read a scripture? Don't beg out of it. Let your yes be your yes, even if on Sunday morning you have a zit the size of a small cantaloupe on the end of your nose. If you've ever been rescued from a terrible situation by God and told him you would be more evangelistic, then be more evangelistic. If you tell your spouse you'll cook dinner three times a week, get your cooking shoes on.

Probably, one of the most difficult things about being a Christian is this idea of letting your yes be your yes and no be your no. It may make you hesitant to make commitments of any kind, but it shouldn't. Let us just become more responsible to others. Jesus kept his word. He said he would rise three days after his death, he did. He healed the people he said he would. He really loved Peter when he said he did, even though Peter did him wrong.

Let us not make fancy oaths and promises and just do what we tell others we're going to do. Let me warn you though, it's much easier said than done.

**Little Eyes Are Watching**

Episode 34 "Beaver's Bad Day" June 4, 1958
Written by John Whedon
Bible Passage: 1 Timothy 4:12
Video Clip: 12:20 - 13:41

Prayer: *Dear God, Help me be the best example to others who are watching me because I am a Christian. Help me do right in the eyes of others, but especially in your eyes. Amen.*

In "Beaver's Bad Day," after Beaver models the suit his mom just brought back from the tailor, she reminds him to change clothes before he goes out to play with Larry Mondello. "And don't go over to where they're building that new house." Beaver answers with a quick, "I won't." But then Larry arrives and the disobeying begins. Without first taking off his good clothes, Beaver and Larry rush over to that new home site looking for slugs.

Of course, Beaver rips his good pants on a nail and this is the beginning of his bad day. If only he hadn't 1) disobeyed his parents by wearing his good clothes out to play 2) played at a construction site he's not allowed to play at and then 3) lied about how he ripped his pants.

Beaver goes home and tells a tale about a dog chasing and biting him. He adds more lies onto that one lie and eventually Ward lectures Beaver on the better points of always telling the truth. His lecture is interrupted when Fred Rutherford calls to ask Ward to come over that evening for a night of playing cards. He sends Beaver up to his room but he instantly stops when he hears Ward tell a tall tale of why he and June cannot go over that evening.

Later, June finishes Ward's lecture to the Beav. June gives Beaver a very good lesson on why he shouldn't lie. She tells Beaver that God is watching us all the time. Beaver processes this and understands her words quite well. But wait, earlier, Ward had lied to Fred Rutherford when asked if he and June were free to play cards that evening. Beaver now understands that God is watching all the time. What he could not understand was why his Dad lied to

Mr. Rutherford and told him they were busy that night simply because Ward didn't want to go play cards. If it was wrong for him to lie, wondered Beaver, why was it okay for his dad to do the same? Beaver asks pointedly, "Did God see Dad when he was talking on the phone with Mr. Rutherford?"

June answers in the affirmative and admits that parents make mistakes sometimes. That was a polite way to say parents lie. Beaver asks his mom if she's going to send Dad to his room and make him take a nap too (Beaver's punishment for the afternoon). She does something even more unbearable for Ward. The next scene shows Ward on the phone with Fred Rutherford saying he and June can now make it to their house that night to play cards. Talk about punishment for Ward, that's a doozy.

God's rules apply to all people, no matter their sex, age, race or status. The principles God wants us to live by are not part of a buffet where we pick one from this column and one from another column and bypass all the ones we don't like. If God says don't tell a lie, that means children shouldn't tell a whopper when they rip their pants like Beaver did while he was doing something he shouldn't have been doing in a place where he shouldn't have been. But it also means parents shouldn't tell a lie to get themselves out of an uncomfortable situation.

June was right. God can see us right though the ceilings of our homes. Even if we hide in a closet, as Beaver proposes, God can see us. There's no hiding from a loving God that wants the best for us but who will also punish us when we do wrong. He's just like a loving parent and we should all take solace in that because although our parents are flawed, they really do want what is best for us. On rare occasions, parents don't always have the best in mind for us, but those occurrences are rare.

**Leaving Home**

Episode 35 "Boarding School" June 11, 1958
Written by Connelly and Mosher Roland MacLane, Dick Conway
Bible Passage: Matthew 19:5
Video Clip: 20:54-23:43

Prayer: *Dear God, Help our world more readily see the real meaning of love and to demonstrate that "real love" to its children. Amen.*

Wally's former classmate is back in town and dropping by for a visit. June announces this as Wally and Beaver are about to go out and play for the day. Now, their day is ruined because of June's invitation to Johnny Franklin. When he arrives at the house, he goes up to the boy's room and he looks like a general addressing his troops. He's in full military regalia, his dress uniform from Bellport Military Academy. He talks about riding horses and shooting guns and having sentry duty. All of this military talk entices Wally to ask his parents if he could attend Bellport Military Academy.

They don't shoot down the idea and even agree to take him up to Bellport to see the school. Wally is very excited to attend until Eddie Haskell shows his smug mug around the Cleaver house. He wants to know why Ward Cleaver wants to get rid of his son. It wasn't their dad's idea say Wally and Beaver. They only thought of it after Johnny Franklin came by to visit. "Oh yeah," says Eddie. "And who invited Johnny Franklin to come over?" That gets Wally thinking.

Over the next few days, Wally's enthusiasm is curbed and his parents can't seem to understand why. Beaver lets the cat out of the bag when he asks his dad why he doesn't like Wally anymore. Ward assures him of his love for Wally and Beaver continues, "Then why are you trying to get rid of him?" After Beaver's intervention, honesty prevails in the Cleaver household and an agreement is made with his dad that Wally may just go next year instead, but he should try Mayfield High first.

There are a lot of kids in this world with parents who make them think they are unwanted. A lot of this can be seen in actual abusive parents. Other times, it can be seen in the ignoring of a child's accomplishments or a child's desire to play catch or do something else with Daddy or Mommy.

Too soon, we are encouraging our kids to leave mother and father, allowing them to be baby sat by television, and I assure you, they aren't watching *Leave it to Beaver* episodes the entire time. If they were, maybe that would be fine. Our kids are put in daycare, immediately upon birth in some cases. Why? Because we've bought into the lies that we as adults need every new electronic gadget, need a bigger house and a new car every three to five years, etc. Our society has bought it all, hook, line and sinker.

Sometimes our children are babysat by neighbors, but what are the neighbor's kids doing to our children? I had a neighbor once who took care of a few kids and I couldn't believe what I saw in the yard next door. The neighbor's kids were teasing one child and encouraging the family dog to do things to him which was enough to traumatize him far into adulthood. Praise God that child had clothes on and shame on me for not marching over there and telling the mother what was going on. Parents should be careful about where, when and how their kids are weaned.

We don't need to be a society where we make sure this biblical concept of leave mother and father begins at age "0" and is exasperated and sped up by junior high. These days, by the time 7th grade rolls around, we've created little independent creatures who demand privacy at all times, want to hide everything they say and do on the internet or their phone.

Kids need to learn to be responsible adults and by the time they are adults, be able to live independently. Yes, teach them how to wash their own clothes by age 8 if you want, cook the family meal by age 12, teach them all about having their own savings and checking accounts, the dangers of credit cards, etc., but don't give them blanket independence with their phones and the internet which has been shown by example after example, to create trouble for youth.

Matthew 19:5 clearly states, "a man will leave his father and mother…" That's great; all parents want that to happen eventually. But what kids really want is to be part of a close, loving family and they want to spend time with their parents, unless of course, their parents have already created a highly independent creature by age 7 or 8.

We sometimes reap what we sow. Every Father's Day, my former minister would read the lyrics to the song, "Cat's in the Cradle," by Harry Chapin. The song is about a father who never had time for his son. As he grew, the son would often say with admiration and a smile, "I'm gonna be like him, yeah, I'm gonna be a lot like him." Beginning in college, the father is slowing down and wants to spend time with his son. But the shoe is on the other foot now, the son is the one who doesn't have time for the father. Time progresses and the song ends with this sad verse:

*I've long since retired, my son's moved away*
*I called him up just the other day*
*I said, I'd like to see you, if you don't mind*
*He said I'd love to Dad, if I can find the time.*
*You see, the new job's a hassle and the kids have the flu*
*but it's sure nice talking to you Dad / It's been sure nice talking to you*
*And as I hung up the phone it occurred to me / he'd grown up just like me*
*My boy was just like me.*

(Okay, I'm in tears)

In this book, this is my one attempt at preaching because I think this is an important message. There's no doubt that God would be pleased if we would simply slow down and spend more time with our families. Can I hear an "Amen?"

# Thou Shall Not

Episode 36 "Beaver and Henry" June 18, 1958
Written by Joe Connelly and Bob Mosher
Bible Verse: Ephesians 4:29
Video Clip: 13:21-16:43

Prayer: *Dear God, Help me be a positive influence in the lives of others instead of focusing only on the negative. It is much easier to be negative, but I know with your power, positivity can flow from my heart and my lips. Amen.*

Something has been chomping down June Cleaver's flowers. She worked so hard planting such pretty flowers and some varmint is eating them for a late night snack. What should Ward do? He fixes a trap to catch that groundhog they believe is eating the petunias and marigolds.  In the early morning hours just as the sun is rising, Wally and Beaver look out their window and see the trap has been sprung. "Dad! Dad!" they yell. Both Ward and June rush down to the yard to see what they've caught. Instead of a groundhog, they discover a white rabbit. They decide to keep it and Beaver names it Henry.

It's an adorable rabbit, but June soon informs Ward that the rabbit would be better suited to be called Henrietta, especially a rabbit in her condition. The Cleaver household will soon have multiple rabbits. Never informing Beaver about the change that's soon to come, you can imagine the trauma he endures when he discovers Henry feeding her babies. This is a must see episode if only for that Beaver moment.

Sometimes in life we get advice that is a day late and a dollar short. In this episode, Beaver receives some advice that is not a dollar short, but is a few minutes too late. Ward advises Beaver, via Wally, not to pick up any of the baby rabbits because the mother could smell a human on it and not nurse it any longer and the baby rabbit might die.

Not knowing what to do and not wanting the baby rabbit to die, Beaver trudges off to the fire station and talks to his friend Gus the fireman. Gus always seems to know how to fix a problem and that's no different with this situation. He advises Beaver to take some talcum powder and rub it on the baby so the mother will not smell the human. He also said that for good measure, he should also dab a bit of vanilla on the nose of the mother to be absolutely certain the mother will not smell human.

Beaver does these things and when Ward discovers the smell of powder, he stops Beaver and asks him about why the rabbit has the aroma of talcum powder. Beaver tells him how he touched the baby rabbit and didn't want the mama to stop nursing it. How did he know to do this wondered Ward. Beaver tells his dad Gus the fireman told him what to do. Of course, this elicited another question from Ward. "Why didn't you come to me to ask what to do?" That's when honesty hits Ward right between the eyes." Beaver says, "Dad, you're better at telling me things not to do, than what to do." Wow! That's a mighty strong indictment on his parenting style.

I think Beaver hit the nail on the head when it comes to some parenting styles and what most people who don't go to church think about the Bible and the church itself. If there is one thing religion has done well throughout history, it's telling people what not to do. "Do not dance." "Do not drink." "Do not cuss." Do not watch R rated movies." "Do not have sex unless you're married." That's a lot of "do not's."

We can hold to beliefs that are in the negative. That's not a problem. We know the Bible and church tells us to not do certain things. However, when we try to tell our friends about Jesus and church for that matter, maybe some of the things we should focus on are the positives, like how much Jesus loves us (John 3:16) how he wants us to have an abundant life (John 10:10), how he wants to help us when we are weary (Matthew 11:28), how he gives us a helper in the Holy Spirit (John 14:26). This list of positives could go on forever.

If you've ever noticed street preachers like the ones I see in downtown Dallas, they haven't changed in the over twenty years I've witnessed them. They are screaming at passersby. They aren't screaming Jesus love you. It's more like a rehash of Jonathan Edwards' sermon, "Children in the Hands of an Angry God." These street preachers are telling those waiting for buses they are going to hell if they don't change their ways. I'm sure they're right in some instances, but they don't know the hearts and souls of each person waiting at the stop.

Beaver was trying to point out that he may like his dad to not always tell him what NOT to do and to maybe be just a little bit more positive of a person when it comes to his parenting style. Of course, Beaver wasn't articulate enough to state it in such a way, maybe his way was even better.

Let's be positive in all our endeavors and leave negativity far behind. It may benefit us in ways we'd never even imagine.

## Going Home

Episode 37 "Beaver Runs Away" June 25, 1958
Written by Joe Connelly and Bob Mosher
Bible Passage: Luke 15:11-32
Video Clip: 12:36 - 14:56

Prayer: *Dear God, For the people in my life who have run away from you, please allow me to gently guide them home. Amen.*

In one of the more emotional *Leave it to Beaver* episodes, Beaver decides to leave home. He even tells his dad that he will run away and his dad will never see him again. Ward tells him to run away if he must. He won't stop him from doing so. Beaver sits on the porch for a while before finally leaving 485 Mapleton and heads over to Larry Mondello's house.

This episode is filled with themes we can find in the Bible. At one point, June tells Beaver not to be afraid of being punished because he knows his dad will be fair. "Yeah, that's what I'm afraid of," he says. There's also the point of exasperating our children, which is something we shouldn't do. Ward doesn't yell at him per se, but he does show his anger and displeasure, more so than in other episodes. When your son threatens to run away, especially a boy as young as Beaver in season one, and you do nothing to stop him, and by not doing anything, you encourage him to leave, that may be "exasperation." Beaver looks very confused when he walks out the door, repeatedly saying goodbye and waiting for his dad to say "don't go" and all Ward does is say, "Goodbye."

After June frantically searches for Beaver throughout the neighborhood and comes up empty, Wally suggests they call the police because Beaver really did run away. Ward suggests they make some calls to his friend's houses first. Larry Mondello is at the top of the list. "Oh," says Ward. "He's just now finishing up his supper." June hears this and goes to get Beaver. Meanwhile, back at the home of a man who may be thinking he made a mistake, has that confirmed by his son Wally.

---

Ward tells Wally that he couldn't let the Beaver win. Wally innocently tells him Beaver doesn't want to win. "Beaver just wants to come back without looking like a creep." Ward has one of those hurtful "ah-ha" moments. A few minutes later Beaver returns and he walks over slowly to his dad. Their conversation centers on Beaver's asking about the time his dad ran away and how he felt when his own dad didn't go out looking for him. Ward answers, "It made me feel pretty bad." Beaver asks a more pointed question next, "Then why didn't you come out looking for me?"

We probably each have family members or friends who have left a congregation or maybe they've left their family and been estranged for some reason or another. Maybe they, like Beaver want to come back to the fold, but they don't want to look like a creep or feel foolish or whatever negative metaphor you may want to use. People have pride and if they have made a bad decision to leave their church or their family, they may have realized they need to go back. That's not an easy thing to admit and we should make it as easy as we can to accept them back into the loving arms of a congregation or a family.

Maybe this someone is you? Maybe you feel like you want to be back in God's family or your own personal family, but you don't know how to take the first step. I know Jesus wants to be of help, and he also has a lot of people in this world that can help in a realistic and heartfelt way. Visit my website http://brianhumek.com/books and send a message via the contact page. Let's get you, your friend, or co-worker back where God wants you, back where you belong.

## Hospitality

Episode 38 "Beaver's Guest" July 2, 1958
Written by Joe Connelly and Bob Mosher
Bible Passage: 1 Peter 4:9
Video Clip: 22:37 – 24:44

Prayer: *Dear God, Thank you for those homes you've allowed me to enter and the eloquent examples of hospitality you've placed into my life. Please help me to be just as hospitable to others as they have been to me. Amen.*

There aren't many things that God likes more than hospitality. We see example after example of it in the pages of the Bible. In fact, a glimpse of BibleGateway.com shows 8447 examples of hospitality in one form or another. The big verse here is 1 Peter 4:9 which says in the NIV Bible, "Offer hospitality to one another without grumbling." I think I like best the way the New Life Bible interprets the verse, "Be happy to have people stay for the night and eat with you."

So far in season one; we've seen examples of hospitality in "Lumpy Rutherford," "New Neighbors," and now here in "Beaver's House Guest." In this episode, Beaver invites Larry to spend the night. The weekend doesn't go entirely as planned. As little kids will do, they fight and Larry insists on leaving, but he and Beaver make up within the hour and the weekend continues. Larry also gets sick after eating too much candy. Ward and June have one exhausting weekend and are reminiscing over it at the supper table after Larry has finally been picked up by his mom.

Ward had promised Wally that he too could have a friend spend the night and Wally asks at supper whether Eddie Haskell could spend the night the next weekend. After some banter and some very nice words from Wally, Ward relents and allows Eddie Haskell to spend the next Friday night with them. Talk about being hospitable, allowing Eddie Haskell to spend the night is the epitome of Jesus saying we should walk the extra mile.

When it comes to the church, I once had a ministry professor tell our class that the churches of Christ are some of the most hospitable in the world. "I've gone all over," he told us. "Travelled the world and I've never had to book a hotel room." My bride and I have noticed this too and still experience it at least once or twice a year[22]. Being welcomed into someone's home, when they don't have some ulterior motive, is one of the nicest feelings in the world.

Remember what Jesus said about feeding someone who is hungry. If we do it for the hungry, we've also done it for Jesus. The same thing goes for hospitality. If we simply welcome someone into our home, whether it's for only one meal, a drink of water, a conversation or to spend the night, whatever we're doing for someone else, we're doing it for Jesus too. Believe it or not, when the Cleaver's were hospitable to Eddie Haskell, they were being hospitable to Jesus also. That's what Jesus said.

When was the last time you had someone into your home and shared a meal or just a conversation? Does your congregation encourage you to be hospitable? Have you ever heard 1Peter 4:9 mentioned from the pulpit or have you heard a sermon on hospitality? We are a busy society. We have been convinced by the advertisers of Madison Avenue that we need to make as much money as possible to have everything imaginable under the sun, but what about friendships, the deeper ones, not the superficial acquaintances we have in our workplaces or at church?

God will be pleased if you invite someone into your home. He's not asking you to invite someone over as annoying as Eddie Haskell, but at least invite someone whose company you enjoy. If your house is too messy, then just invite someone over to your local pizza joint. And remember, no grumbling, that's what God is calling us to do.

---

[22] We witnessed hospitality first in our friend Margaret in Abilene, Texas. She's the epitome of a gracious Christian host who does not grumble.

## Continuity

Episode 39 "Cat Out of the Bag" July 16, 1958
Written by Connelly & Mosher, Dick Conway, Roland MacLane
Bible Passage: All 66 Books of the Bible
Video Clip: 2:36-4:39

Prayer: *Dear God, Thank you for the consistency you have provided in the Bible and in my life. I need stability in my life and you provide it. Amen.*

I think the producers and writers of *Leave it to Beaver* must have known I would write this book one day. They knew I was going to search for some Biblical truth in each episode and write devotional thoughts inspired by their work. Why else would they create an episode, the final one of the first season, and have absolutely nothing within it to relate to the church, Bible or God himself?

I think they did it so I could point to something even bigger. I'm jesting of course, but because I could not stretch any Bible truth to cover Beaver and Wally taking care of a neighbor's cat, I decided to focus on something very important and very reassuring for Christians. What better way to end this book?

There's something all true *Leave it to Beaver* fans know about the series. There is often times a lack of continuity. In today's episode, an example is Mr. Donaldson. He is played by actor Ray Kellogg, but twenty episodes earlier; he was played by a younger actor named Charles Gray. Their personalities also seem to be different. The first was lean and tough while the second Mr. Donaldson was taller, bigger and more of a gentle giant who loved his kitty cat.

There are many inconsistencies and examples of a lack of continuity on the show. Look at Ward Cleaver who works with Fred Rutherford. They are good friends, and Ward didn't know Lumpy was his son in episode #16. The Cleavers live at 485 Mapleton in most episodes during seasons 1 & 2 but there are times when their address is 485 Maple. What about Wally? He enters high school in season two and stays there for a total of five years, but nowhere does it say within the series, that he failed. The only one who is mentioned to have failed is Lumpy.

These inconsistencies in *Leave it to Beaver* (and many other shows) are what one calls, "a lack of continuity." There are many more examples of this in what I call the greatest classic TV comedy, but I'll let you discover those on your own.

The reassurance I would like to leave you with is this, with God and his story, there is no lack of continuity. He's the same from beginning to end. His story was given to us over a period of over 1500 years by 40 different authors who themselves, had different backgrounds from a guy like Habakkuk who did landscape work (a nipper of sycamore trees) to Moses who was a political leader and Paul who was a persecutor of Christians who wrote thirteen of the New Testament books.

The story God gave us doesn't show him changing, no matter how much detractors to Christianity would like to say it does. He was a God of grace in the Old Testament, always giving the disobedient ways to repent. God showed his love for humans from page one in Genesis to the last page of Revelation. He loved mankind and after Adam and Eve decided to leave the perfect life God gave them, the rest of his story deals with how mankind could get back into a "right" position with Him.

This is a simplistic explanation, but in reality, the Bible is mighty simple to understand. I don't believe people can merely gloss over the violence and death seen in the Old Testament, but those situations do not make God a mean God. It shows he is the Holy God, the one and only God that cannot look upon evil and let it stand. All sin must be punished. He pleads through the prophets, for people to turn from their wicked ways. Sometimes they do, like in Nineveh. Sometimes they don't like in Sodom and Gomorrah.

God is the same, yesterday, today and tomorrow. He will punish us when we do wrong. That has never changed. He will love us always. He will never forsake us, even when we forsake him. The ultimate example of continuity is definitely not *Leave it to Beaver*. The ultimate example of continuity is our Father, God.

## Conclusion

One of the better known songs in the 1960s Disney movie *Mary Poppins*, was "A Spoonful of Sugar Helps the Medicine Go Down." You may have already realized it, but that is exactly what you've just experienced through the pages of *Leave it to God*. The *medicine* in this case was God's word, the truth given to us by our Creator. The *sugar* was the *Leave it to Beaver* references within each devotional and the Beaver Tidbit sections. Depending on where you are in your walk with Christ, you may feel like you now have a cavity or you may be thinking, "Mmmmm, that was tasty."

The main takeaways I hope you leave this devotional section with are that God loves you, He wants the best for you and that Christians should treat people with love and respect. Even though those items are not always evident in our lives, they are true. Despite the fact you've just read devotionals that speak about such things doesn't mean you will totally understand or experience them.

There will be days when you don't feel loved by God, days when everything goes wrong and then, something else bad happens. I'm sure you've experienced those days, haven't you? Sometimes the bad happens because we make bad choices. Other times the bad happens because we simply live in a world that is fallen, a world that was perfect with no problems until Adam and Eve messed it up on page two of the Bible. Stuff just happens sometimes. But please don't think for a moment that God wants you to feel that pain which bad days cause you. He is on your side, rooting for you waiting for you to come to Him and talk.

And if you have experienced fellow Christians who have not shown you love and respect, I apologize. Just like Jesus when he walked this world 2000 years ago and experienced hunger, anger and exhaustion, Christians also experience human frailties just like people who aren't followers of Christ. Christians are sometimes short-tempered, short-sighted, angry, disrespectful, and uncaring, all things Christians shouldn't be, but sometimes are. This short list above are just some of my own personal flaws and as a Christian, I ask God for forgiveness quite often for not treating others the way I should.

I hope as you and I both read these devotionals and re-read them, that not only will we have our brains filled with *Leave it to Beaver* trivia, but that our hearts will soften and accept some of God's truth which we may have been neglecting in our lives.

Well, I gotta go, time to watch "Wally's Haircomb," my all-time favorite *Leave it to Beaver* episode. Please visit brianhumek.com/books and send a message via my contact page to let me know your favorite *Leave it to Beaver* episode or the episode you watched most recently.

# Encyclopedia
# of
# Season One Actors

## The Cleaver Family

**Mathers, Jerry** (b. June 2, 1948) Theodore "Beaver" Cleaver

Jerry Mathers was the consummate child actor. He had a knack from the very beginning for remembering his lines. Directors and producers were amazed at his ability. Jerry wasn't pushed into acting by his mother like so many child actors of the 1950s and 1960s were. It all began quite naturally while shopping for clothes at a big Los Angeles department store somewhere in the San Fernando Valley, possibly at a Desmond's Department Store.

While shopping for clothes, Jerry's mother was approached by a woman who said he looked just like a boy in the family featured in their store catalog. The woman asked if she would allow Jerry to model clothes for them. Mrs. Mathers wasn't quite sure about this offer, but when told it came with cash considerations and free clothes, she assured the woman Jerry could do that modeling job. The rest is history. After many times walking down a runway with a stunning model holding his hand, Jerry grew accustomed to working in front of live audiences. This came in very handy while working on TV with their live studio audiences.[23]

Not soon after the modeling job, Jerry made his way to the NBC show *Four Star Revue,* a variety show which featured a rotation of four hosts. These hosts included Jimmy Durante, Danny Thomas, Jack Carson and Ed Wynn. The show later changed its name to *All-Star Revue* when it began featuring additional hosts. It was on this

---

[23] Interview with Jerry Mathers by Gary Rutowski.

TV show where Jerry Mathers' stock as an actor rose to great heights, a very impressive feat seeing that it was his first TV appearance ever… and he was only two years old.[24]

On the *Four Star Revue*, Jerry's first TV acting job, he walked through a set of swinging doors and into a saloon wearing a diaper, a ten gallon hat and a holster with two six guns. Cowboys were fighting, throwing chairs, breaking bottles over heads. The scene was total chaos. It was live TV and Jerry was calm as could be and a cowboy picked him up and placed him on the bar. Then Jerry recited his first televised lines ever as he slams his little hands down on the bar, "I'm the toughest hombre in these parts, and you'd better have my brand!" Ed Wynn, who played the bartender, placed PET Milk on the bar for Jerry and began his schpeel for the sponsor.

After his calm portrayal of this little cowboy, bottles and chairs flying all around him, Jerry became popular with directors of early TV shows like *The Ray Bolger Show* and *December Bride*, among many others. His popularity was due in part because there were very few child actors in Los Angeles at the time, and fewer still who could recite lines and not be frightened in front of a live audience. His intelligence helped with the first, his experience as a model helped with the second. One such show interested in working with Jerry was *Lux Video Theater*, the television version of the very famous and long lasting *Lux Radio Theater* which had starred host Cecile B. DeMille. While filming *Lux Video Theater*, Jerry was seen by Alfred Hitchcock who was present on the set to promote his latest film, *To Catch a Thief*. [25]

---

[24] In the Archives of American Television interview conducted on June 20, 2006 Jerry mentions his first job in television as an advertisement for Pet Milk on the Colgate Comedy Hour, but adds "or some variety show." In this interview he is not certain which show, but on many websites you will find it listed as definitely being the Colgate Comedy Hour. However, further research has shown that Pet Milk sponsored the Four Star Revue on NBC in 1950 and on that series, Ed Wynn was a host and did a commercial for Pet Milk. Most likely, this is the one featuring Jerry Mathers as a little cowboy.

Alfred Hitchcock saw Jerry's performance and like everyone else in early 1950s Hollywood, was impressed with the maturity and acting abilities of the young Jerry Mathers. He offered Jerry a role in his next film *The Trouble with Harry*, originally an experiment by Hitchcock in making a film without a star lead and featuring more subtle humor.[26] Two years later, Jerry was cast as the lead in *Leave it to Beaver* and it all began with a modeling job when he was two years old. That job prepared him for live TV which was a springboard to his role in an Alfred Hitchcock movie, eventually leading Jerry to his new agent Glen Shaw who encouraged he try out for the role of The Beaver.

The show for which Jerry Mathers is most famous lasted on television for six seasons. The first season, the one featured in this book, aired on CBS but due to ratings which weren't as high as CBS execs had hoped for, was cancelled. The situation comedy was then picked up by ABC where it aired in numerous nights and time slots until 1963. Due to its popularity today, many fans believe *Leave it to Beaver* was a huge hit during its original run, but it never did crack the top 30 shows from 1957-1963. The show always had stiff competition which included shows such as *The Defenders* during season five, while season six saw it compete against the likes of *Perry Mason* and *Dr. Kildare*.

*Leave it to Beaver* was not cancelled at the end of the sixth season. The cast was asked by the brass at ABC if they wanted to continue the show for another two or three year commitment and Jerry declined. He wanted to live a life like all other boys his age. He wanted to attend a real high school, play sports and maybe start a band. That last desire may not have been mentioned in his official decline of ABC's offer, but it is what happened a few years later when Jerry Mathers and Richard Correll (Richard Rickover on *Leave it to Beaver*) began a band named *Beaver and the Trappers*.

---

[25] In the same interview, Jerry states Alfred Hitchcock was "promoting his latest film." Hitchcock's latest film at that time was *It Takes a Thief* and he next made *The Trouble with Harry* in which he cast Jerry Mathers in his biggest role up to that time.

[26] "Trouble with Harry", IMDB.com, accessed September 17, 2014.

---

Jerry never lost the acting bug. Immediately after high school he had roles on *Batman*, *Lassie*, and *My Three Sons* but his career went on hiatus while in the Air Force, the Air International Guard and in college at the University of California at Berkley where he graduated with a degree in Philosophy. He later went on to work in banking and real estate before getting back into acting in a stage play with his television brother Tony Dow in *Boing, Boing* which ran for 8 weeks and he later had a successful run on the dinner theater circuit for 17 continuous months in the comedy *So Long, Stanley*.

After their success in *So Long, Stanley*; Jerry and Tony knew there was an audience for them and it wasn't much longer until others in Hollywood figured the same. In 1983, *Still the Beaver* was produced and was met with so much success that the reunion movie *Still the Beaver* was spun off into a re-boot of the *Leave it to Beaver* television series. This time the show was called *Still the Beaver* and aired on the Disney Channel for one year. Cancelled after its debut season, the show moved to Superstation TBS for the following three seasons. Jerry starred in all 102 episodes and many of the cast of the original series joined him. Huge exceptions included Hugh Beaumont (died in 1982 of a heart attack), Stanley Fafara (the original Whitey Whitney), and Stephen Talbot (Gilbert Bates).

Since the end of *The New Leave it to Beaver*, Jerry Mathers has gained even more fame around the world for his role as Beaver Cleaver. In 1980 the show was shown in over 20 countries and translated into 15 different languages.[27] A quarter of a century later, the show was televised in 127 countries and Jerry's words were translated or subtitled in over 91 languages.[28] As Jerry often says, "I can go anywhere in the world, and people know me."[29] Notice his words carefully. He spoke in the positive. He cherishes the role which made him a household name with worldwide fame and that is commendable.

---

[27] Pattie Reilly, "Leave It to Beaver: Tony Dow and Jerry Mathers Find a New Channel for Their Talent—Dinner Theater,"*People*, May 05,1980.

[28] Jerry Mathers, interviewed by Gary Rutkowski.

[29] Campbell Robertson, And Jerry Mathers as... Tracy Turnblad's Father?, *New York Times*, June 5, 2007.

Jerry Mathers continues to act. His last role was in *The Hitchhiker* a short film released in 2014. He is also a very in demand speaker for corporate events and is a spokesman for diabetes awareness, having become inflicted with diabetes in 1996. He has since, with exercise and diet, gotten his diabetes under control and is now pre-diabetic.

Wherever he goes and in whatever he does, Jerry Mathers is a goodwill ambassador spreading smiles as he travels down this long road called life. Whatever his religious persuasion, I would have to say he is a living example of how Christians should act in this world.

## Dow, Tony (b. 1945) Wally Cleaver

A very talented athlete, Tony Dow was much more interested in sports, specifically swimming and diving when he was a child, than he was in acting. He had won a junior Olympic championship and was a Western States champion diver. His athletic abilities came to him by way of his mother, Muriel Montrose. She was a stunt woman in early cowboy movies, a stand in for silent screen star Clara Bow and was also a Mack Sennett Bathing Beauty. Instead of pushing her son Tony into acting like many "stage" mothers were known for, Tony's mother encouraged him to swim and dive.[30]

It was because of his swimming and diving expertise that he got a break on the small screen. A lifeguard, a beginning actor named Bill Bryant [31], at The Hollywood Athletic Club where Tony practiced his swimming, encouraged him to go along to a TV show audition. The pilot was for *Johnny Wildlife* and the lifeguard was going to audition for the part of a father and Tony would audition for the part of his son. Tony agreed and earned the part but his friend the

---

[30] Clifford Terry, "Tony Dow: Living with Depressive Illness," *Baltimore Sun*, August 1, 1993, accessed September 26, 2014,**http://articles.baltimoresun.com/1993-08-01/features/1993213175_1_depression-tony-dow-sweet-simplicity.**

[31] Tony Dow, interviewed by Eric Greenburg.

lifeguard came away from the audition empty handed.[32] Needless to say, since Tony Dow wound up doing *Leave it to Beaver*, the *Johnny Wildlife* series did not go into production.

It wasn't long before Tony did contract a little of the acting bug and secured other auditions, one of those being for *Leave it to Beaver*. In an interview with Eric Greenburg for his "Just My Show" podcast, Tony explained that the executive producer for *Johnny Wildlife*, Harry Ackerman, was also the executive producer for *Leave it to Beaver* and encouraged Tony to go for the audition.[33] Not yet titled *Leave it to Beaver*, this audition was for an older brother on a situation comedy called *Wally and the Beaver*.

Many of the other actors had already been cast. However, the part of Wally, which had been played by actor Paul Sullivan in the pilot episode, "It's a Small World," was being re-cast because after the pilot and before production of the first episode, Sullivan had grown about six inches, no longer looking like a big brother but like a college basketball player.[34] Without regard to height, Tony Dow was a much better fit to be Beaver's big brother. There was chemistry between the two and Tony, despite having no acting credits except for a bit part on *NBC's Children Theater* in 1949 as a four year old, was a much better actor than the original Wally.

Tony Dow was the perfect big brother. Everyone in America seemed to wish he was theirs. He became more popular as the seasons progressed, having more story lines feature him and raising his star power among American teenage girls. After *Leave it to Beaver*, he appeared on *Mr. Novak, Dr. Kildare* and *My Three Sons* and acted regularly in the soap opera, *Never Too Young*. He then took a hiatus from acting after entering the National Guard in 1965.

In the 1970s, Tony continued to act but also started a successful small construction firm. Toward the end of the decade, Tony asked his television brother Jerry Mathers to join him in a production of

---

[32] According to IMDB.com, actor Bill Bryant went onto a long Hollywood career with over 200 acting credits.

[33] Tony Dow interviewed by Eric Greenburg.

[34] Jerry Mathers interviewed by Gary Rutkowski.

the play, *Boing, Boing,* which had an eight week run in Kansas City, Missouri. The production sold out in days. After that success, both he and Jerry starred in a production of the comedy *So Long, Stanley.* This production lasted 17 months as it toured the country to sold out audiences.

In 1983, the Beaver cast reunited for the TV movie, *Still the Beaver* and its success brought on an effort to revive their TV series which had ended over 20 years earlier. The new show was titled, "*The New Leave it to Beaver.*" There were 102 episodes of the show, and Tony directed five of its episodes in 1988 and 1989. Tony sharpened his directing skills and was in much demand in the early 1990s working on such shows as *Get a Life, Harry and the Hendersons, Swamp Thing, Coach* and *Babylon Five.*

By 2003, Tony had begun taking his lifelong passion of sculpting more seriously and relied less and less on Hollywood for accolades and his self-esteem. Knowing for years Hollywood was becoming more of a young kids' game, being run by young executives and producers, it became a game he didn't want to play. He first noticed this while on an audition and a 28 year old executive asked, "Have you ever done comedy before?" That's when Tony thought to himself, "Hmmm, maybe it is time for me to retire. Maybe it is time to take the art seriously."[35]

Specifically, his art is semi-abstract burl wood and bronze sculptures. He finds the burl wood in the woods of Topanga Canyon which surround his home. He spends a lot of time searching for this fallen wood and in his studio making creations which have found admiration throughout the world. In 2008, one of his pieces was featured in an exhibit in the famed Louvre Art Museum in Paris, France.

His sculptures are represented by the DeBilzan Gallery in Laguna Beach where Tony will have an occasional show. Other galleries which feature his sculptures are Stephano's Fine Art Gallery in Little Rock, Arkansas and the Wilde Meyer Gallery which

---

[35] John Rogers, "Beav's Brother Tony Dow Now an Abstract Artist," The Big Story, September 22, 2012, accessed September 29, 2014, http://bigstory.ap.org/article/beavs-brother-tony-dow-now-abstract-artist.

has locations in Scottsdale and Tuscon, AZ. You can learn more about his sculptures at tonydowsculpture.com[36]. My favorite of his sculptures is his bronze, "Looking for God," so please, tell everyone to buy multiple copies of this book to give as birthday and Christmas gifts so I can afford that purchase. His sculptures are pieces of fine art, so they are quite pricey, but are well worth every dollar.

Although Tony may not have small or large screen acting credits listed on IMDB in the past few years, he continues to love acting and directing, but does so on a more intimate level, doing so for smaller stage audiences. In 2009 he toured with Judy Norton in the production of *Love Letters*, a Pulitzer Prize winning play, which made its successful tour in various cities. It was so popular that some areas had Judy and Tony back in 2010 for repeat performances and in 2012 Tony toured with the play with actress Joyce DeWitt.

Tony Dow always has and always will be an artist, whether his art manifests itself in his brilliant sculptures or in his amazing acting abilities; that all depends on the venue.

**Beaumont, Hugh** (1907-1982) Ward Cleaver

Hugh Beaumont is a parental hero to many people. His portrayal of an idyllic father on *Leave it to Beaver* was and still is much loved because of the unyielding patience he demonstrated with his children and their repeated problems. Okay, maybe not so much patience when doing homework with Beaver, but otherwise, Ward Cleaver was a very patient man.

In real life, he was a very patient man too and quite caring, a centerpiece of his Christianity as Hugh Beaumont, as many may not know, was a Methodist lay minister for years before earning a Masters of Theology degree from USC in 1946. He remained a Methodist and dedicated to church work throughout his life. He also played the role of a clergyman on TV and in the movies ten different times; the most prominent was on *The Lone Ranger* episode,

[36] "Sales," Tony Dow Sculpture, accessed September 29, 2014, http://www.tonydowsculpture.com/sales/.

"Godless Men," from the show's third season. He even wrote a short story for the *Saturday Evening Post* in 1951 titled, "Reverend Telford's Failure."[37]

While already doing work in theater and radio, he did not turn to acting in movie roles until after his marriage to actress Kathryn Adams in 1940. At that time, because the congregation where he worked could barely afford to pay him, he needed extra funds to supplement his income and he found this extra income through work on the big screen.[38] Others have reported he worked in movies to only help pay for extra church programs needed for his congregation.

"Sometimes my work as an actor presents a conflict with my ideals as a clergyman. I don't believe in the old saying that the end justifies the means, and no money that I can earn as an actor can accomplish so much good that I would feel justified in violating my ideals to earn it… If the question ever arises in a serious way, of course I would have to give up my acting."[39]

The above quote could be seen in action in one of his more popular roles, that of detective Michael Shayne. Beginning in 1940 actor Lloyd Nolan brought this hardboiled detective from radio and turned him into a popular character on the big screen via seven films for 20th Century Fox. In his film portrayal and in the original Shayne books, Michael Shayne was not adverse to physical violence to get his way with a bad guy. But in the Michael Shayne films featuring Hugh Beaumont beginning in 1946, according to various IMDB reviews, Beaumont's Michael Shayne is more easy going, pleasant and likes to crack jokes, somewhat similar to Dick Powell's portrayal on radio of Detective Richard Diamond sans the singing. But true to all 1940s "B" detective movies, he does inflict harm via his fists on movie antagonists when he must.

[37] "Hugh Beaumont" IMDB.com.

[38] Jerry Mathers, interviewed by MeTV Monitor, January 28, 2014, MeTVnetwork.com.

[39] Hugh Beaumont Obituary *Associated Press*, May 16, 1982.

A role much better suited for his personality, one that would fit his Christian religion would wind up being the father Ward Cleaver in *Leave it to Beaver*. This does not mean to say he immediately loved the role, as situation comedy was looked down upon by many serious actors at the time. But he did, according to Barbara Billingsley, come to admire the role of Ward Cleaver over time. [40] Playing Ward also helped typecast Hugh as well as all *Leave it to Beaver* actors for a time period after the series ended. This is never enjoyable for actors who want to branch out to a broader range of acting after a successful series.

After *Leave it to Beaver*, Hugh Beaumont acted in bit roles, many in dramas such as *The Virginian, Marcus Welby M.D., Mannix, Medical Center* and *Wagon Train*. In 1972 he suffered a stroke, from which doctors thought he might not recover. However, Hugh surprised the pessimistic docs and returned to live an active life as a Christmas tree farmer in Minnesota and he still did a little work in local theater.

Hugh Beaumont suffered a heart attack in 1982 while visiting his son Hunter, a professor living in Germany. He passed away one year before the reunion movie *Still the Beaver* was filmed. It would have been a tremendous blessing if Ward Cleaver could have been part of that movie and the subsequent series.

In ministry most of his life, I hope Hugh Beaumont would've been proud to know that his words and understanding ways presented to the world through the character Ward Cleaver, are making a difference in people's lives today through the devotionals in this book.

## Billingsley, Barbara (1906-2010) June Cleaver

One week after turning the ripe old age of 22, Barbara made her way to Broadway. She arrived in New York City just before the end of 1937 with a stage show she had been part of in Los Angeles titled *The Straw Hat*. The show ran on Broadway from December 30, 1937

---

[40] Barbara Billingsley interviewed by Karen Herman.

to January 1, 1938 for a total of four performances.[41] While the play focused on a female lead (Sylvia Leigh) in a New Hampshire summer stock theater who desired more than anything to be discovered by Hollywood, Barbara did not have that immediate desire and stayed in New York after the play closed. She earned her living in New York as a fashion model. She also toured in the play *Accidentally Yours* with Billie Burke, who is best known for her role as the Good Witch of the North in *The Wizard of Oz*.

Signing her first movie contract in 1945 (MGM), Barbara, now married to restaurateur Glenn Billingsley, moved west to Hollywood. For many years, she played in small roles in "B" movies, oftentimes uncredited. She eventually made her way to bigger films, yet, the roles were still small. Two of those bigger films were *Three Guys Named Mike* starring Jane Wyman and *The Bad and the Beautiful* starring Kirk Douglas, Lana Turner and Dick Powell.

In 1957 Barbara landed her dream role. "I used to lie in bed at night and say, 'Now what would I like to do? I want my children to be proud of it. I want my children to be able to look at it. I used to dream about a show like Beaver. Don't figure that dreams don't come true, because they do," she once told an interviewer.[42] One day she was filming on the set of *Leave it to Beaver* and she had an epiphany, "This is the show I always wanted to do." She also says in that interview that Hugh Beaumont did not come into the series with the same feelings she had. He had wanted to do the show and then move on which was in stark contrast to Barbara who was where she finally wanted to be. Eventually, during the show's run, Hugh Beaumont, she admits, came to greatly appreciate *Leave it to Beaver* for the high quality family show it was. [43]

After *Leave it to Beaver*, Barbara stayed out of the limelight for many years, except for two appearances on the crime drama, *The FBI*. Her preference was to stay at home in Malibu or travel the

---

[41] Thomas S. Hischak, *Broadway Plays and Musicals* (Jefferson, NC: McFarland and Co. Inc., 2009), 441.

[42] Interview with Barbara Billingsley by Karen Herman.

[43] ibid

world with her husband William Mortensen. But in 1980, she came back to the screen, thanks to the producers of *Airplane*, a parody of all those 1970s airline disaster movies. In that film,she portrayed a woman who translated jive for a flight attendant who couldn't understand two men in need of help.

It wasn't three years later until she starred in, *Still the Beaver*, the *Leave it to Beaver* TV movie, and one year after that when she starred in *The New Leave it to Beaver*. Barbara wasn't finished with TV after the second incarnation of *Leave it to Beaver* ended. She went on to do some small parts on TV in *Parker Lewis Can't Lose*, *Empty Nest* and *Murphy Brown*. Her last role came in the 2003 TV movie *Secret Santa*.

In the years after the original *Leave it to Beaver* series, Barbara Billingsley became close friends with her two television sons from the show and also with Ken Osmond (Eddie Haskell) and Frank Bank (Lumpy). Tony Dow and his family seem to have been the closest with Barbara as they ate dinners together once a month for many years. She loved them all and many times reunited with the four actors for TV interviews, *Leave it to Beaver* retrospectives and other public appearances.

Barbara Billingsley died at her Santa Monica home in 2010 after a long illness at the age of 94.

# Beaver and Wally's Friends

**Stevens, Robert "Rusty"** (b. 1948)   Larry Mondello

Playing one of the most popular characters on *Leave it to Beaver* during its first three seasons, and two episodes in season four, Rusty Stevens seemed destined for a long Hollywood career. After a couple acting credits, one when he was only three years old for the TV show *Racket Squad* (a show Hugh Beaumont later narrated), Rusty Stevens went on an audition for *Leave it to Beaver* and won the part of a friend of the main character Beaver.

Rusty Stevens was a very good actor and played the part of a best friend perfectly. His character was also a very annoying student during class time whether for Miss Canfield or Miss Landers and wound up in the principal's office quite often. One of his memorable scenes is in the episode "Beaver's Ring" when after Miss Landers leaves the room to take Beaver to see the school nurse, Larry gets on top of a desk to reach the classroom clock and moves the hands forward so they could get out of class earlier. He steps down from the desk and says, "If anyone squeals on me, I'll punch them right in the nose." Talk about a school bully, but in reality, no one was scared of him because he wound up in the principal's office anyway that afternoon.

Larry was seen quite often in *Leave it to Beaver*. In season one, Rusty made 13 appearances as Beaver's classmate and best friend. That was one third of the episodes that season. In season two, Rusty appeared in 26 of the 39 episodes. In season three he appeared in 25 of the 39 episodes. In season four, Rusty only appeared in the fourth and sixth episodes. His biggest hiatus from the show before leaving entirely in 1960 was when he didn't appear in the last eight episodes in season three and the first five episodes on season four.

Rusty didn't outgrow his role. His voice didn't begin squeaking. He didn't grow a beard at 12 years old. As Barbara Billingsley revealed on her Archives of American TV interview, "We all loved Rusty so much. He was so good in that role. But unfortunately, they had to let him go because of his mother. She'd be up in the producers' office and make demands and everything so they finally let him go."[44] Many *Leave it to Beaver* fans wish Larry would've stayed on the series. It was very sad to see him go.

Continuing with his career for three more years, Rusty Stevens made appearances on some popular early 60s TV shows, among those were, *My Three Sons*, *National Velvet*, *Perry Mason*, *Wagon Train* and his final appearance for over twenty years was on *The Rifleman* in which he played a bully and beat up Lucas McCain's son Mark. That was some rough and tumble fight scene. It looked like either one of those two actors could've been hurt. After that role, Rusty did not show up on the small screen again until his part in the *Leave it to Beaver* reunion movie, *Still the Beaver* in 1983.

Rusty almost didn't appear in *Still the Beaver* because producers of the movie could not find him. A detective was employed to find him and eventually he turned up in New Jersey. He was an insurance salesman near Atlantic City. When the detective knocked on his door, Rusty's wife answered and when asked if the Rusty Stevens who played Larry Mondello on *Leave it to Beaver* lived there, she told the detective he had the wrong house. But Rusty corrected the misunderstanding and told her it was him. He had simply, in all their years of marriage, neglected to tell her he had been a child actor.

*The New Leave it to Beaver* could've been a revival of Rusty's acting career, but he only had three acting credits on the show and after *The New Leave it to Beaver* left the air in 1989, Rusty Stevens was never heard from again. But still today, people are searching for him and there are all sorts of rumors on the internet about what he is doing. As of this first printing of *Leave it to God*, Rusty is now 66 years old and retired, living in southeastern New Jersey in a very nice planned community.

Larry Mondello is still a favorite *Leave it to Beaver* character of many fans. I hope he understands he's part of a treasured past so many people love and that he gains new fans every day and is popular all around the world, due in part to international syndication. God bless Robert "Rusty" Stevens,

---

[44] Barbara Billingsley interviewed Karen Herman.

his immediate family, and his extended family in all their endeavors.

## Fafara, Stanley (1949-2003) Whitey Whitney

Only the actors who portrayed the Cleaver family members, Eddie Haskell and Larry Mondello appeared more often on *Leave it to Beaver* than did Stanley Fafara. He acted in 57 episodes and was mentioned in many others. These mentions either occurred as a telephone call from Whitey or at other times he was mentioned as someone Beaver would play with outside. His most memorable episode was "In the Soup" from season four. In this episode, Whitey and Beaver are walking to Whitey's house where Beaver is to spend the night. On their way over, they pass a billboard with a lady holding a steaming cup of soup. Whitey makes a bet with Beaver that there's soup in the cup. Beaver says there isn't and at Whitey's taunting, Beaver climbs up and gets stuck in the cup of soup.

Before *Leave it to Beaver*, Fafara acted in a few commercials and had only previously appeared once on the small screen in a role on *Casey Jones* and once on the big screen, his debut, in the much respected 20th Century Fox release *Good Morning, Miss Dove*. He had a few other appearances during the run of *Leave it to Beaver*, but none afterward.

Fafara, who was the younger brother of another recurring cast member, Tiger Fafara (Tooey Brown), after leaving the show, attended North Hollywood High School. He was urged by his parents to attend a Christian school and he rebuffed their advice, years later admitting, "I think one of my downfalls was not listening to my parents."[45] While at North Hollywood High, he fell in with a popular crowd and enjoyed more than the occasional party. The fast life caught up with Stan (as he preferred to be called) when he befriended the guys in the 60s rock band Paul Revere and the Raiders. He became involved in drugs in the mid-60s finally

---

[45] Stanley Fafara, emailed to Tim Schmitt, August 10, 1998.

becoming clean and sober in 1995 after many failed attempts at sobriety.

In 1998, through an email correspondence with Tim Schmitt, the founder of leaveittobeaver.org, Fafara spoke about a book he was writing about his life and said it was a story about a man who seemed to throw his life away only to eventually find the "loving powerful hand of God," the one thing he, himself had been searching for all along.[46] Stan admits in one email, "That is what happened to me. I just took the long way home." He also, in a later email, talks about the brutal honesty the book would contain. Unfortunately, the 100 pages he had finished in 1998 have never surfaced for his fans to read.

Stan Fafara died in 2003 after complications from surgery on an intestine constricted by a hernia. Seven friends surrounded him in his hospital room as he passed, one commented on the moment, "We were all holding hands. He was a good man who had the ability to see beyond people's sordid pasts and see the good in everyone. He will be missed."[47]

## Weil, Jeri  (b.1948) Judy Hensler

Playing the arch nemesis of Beaver Cleaver must have been fun for Jeri Weil, and it looked like it was just that. She did a great job as an actress because Jerry Mathers has said many times, to many different people, whether in a formal interview or to fans at personal appearances, that Jeri Weil, the actress who portrayed Judy, was a very nice person. One can tell a good actor or actress simply by how much they differ in real life from their character.

Jeri Weil made her acting debut in the big screen gangster thriller *Because of You*, starring Loretta Young and Jeff Chandler. Her next role was also uncredited, but the stars in the movie were bigger and

---

[46] Stanley Fafara, emailed to Tim Schmitt, August 10, 1998.

[47] Tom Hallman Jr., "Stanley Fafara Obituary," LITB.com, September 26, 2003, accessed September 10, 2014, http://www.litb.com/obit.htm accessed September 10, 2014.

brighter, as in the male lead of John Wayne and his leading lady Donna Reed. The TV shows she appeared on before *Leave it to Beaver* were *Lux Video Theater* (Jerry Mathers appeared on one episode too) and *I Led Three Lives*, a popular anti-Communist show in the 1950s.

In 1957, Jeri beat out many other little girls for the role of Judy Hensler. She had a knack for getting under the skin of Beaver Cleaver. She also ruffled the feathers of the other boys at Grant Avenue School too. Larry and Whitey also couldn't stand her smug attitude and tattletale ways. Knowing she was in reality a very nice person, demonstrates that she, like Ken Osmond (Eddie Haskell) could play a part very different than her real life persona.

A staple on the show from its beginning, Jeri left after the third episode of season four. She never acted on the small or big screen again. She left the show about the same time as Rusty Stevens (Larry Mondello), but for entirely different reasons. While Rusty Stevens had to depart because of a pushy stage mother who continually made demands of the producers and offered her two cents where it was not wanted,[48] Jeri simply grew into the role of a lifetime, that of a beautiful young woman.

While her professional acting career ended, she never ceased being a creative woman. She is a writer, a gardener, an artist and an "old hippy"[49] at heart. Her semi-autobiographical books, a set of three, are stories that are conveyed through the different cars she has owned over the years; a 1961 MG Roadster, a 1973 Super Beetle Convertible (which she still owns) and a 2001 Audi Avant.[50] Jeri is full of life and energy and is accessible through her Facebook page. Go add her as a friend on Facebook and see if she doesn't return the favor. She still lives in sunny Southern California and over the years has sold real estate in the Studio City area of Los Angeles.

---

[48] Barbara Billingsley interviewed by Karen Herman.

[49] Jeri Weil, "Jeri Weil," LITB.com, accessed September 17, 2014, http://www.litb.com/jeriweil.htm.

[50] Ibid.

## Mittelstaedt, Robert (b.1947)   Charles Fredericks

Born and raised in Tujunga, California, Robert Mittelstaedt was the son of a Lutheran pastor. A parishioner in the church where his father pastored was an actress, something not unheard of in Southern California. She had provided her agent's name to Robert's father and living on a meager minister's salary, he thought getting his son into acting could help the family budget. Robert's salary went into the total family budget, but he, himself, took away much more money from his work than he would have made delivering papers or mowing lawns on the weekends.

It wasn't long after obtaining an agent that his father began taking Robert on auditions for commercials, films and TV shows. "I probably did 25 casting interviews for every job I landed," said the former actor in a recent interview. Robert went on to recount the most fun part of the interview process, "My dad would take me to the Brown Derby for chicken pot pie after the interviews. It was cool leaving school early to drive the hour or two to Hollywood, which is what it took pre-freeways."[51]

Before landing his first big part in the pilot episode for the Broderick Crawford vehicle, *Highway Patrol*, Robert had landed parts in numerous TV commercials, including one for Lava Soap. He was on the set for three days for the *Highway Patrol* pilot, earning himself a whopping $104.00. That was a huge sum back in 1955, about $907 in today's money. Robert still has the check today.

The auditions for *Leave it to Beaver* were tedious and lasted a long time, longer than for any other role he auditioned for at that time. The casting, he says, "went on for six months and it came down to me and Jerry Mathers. He got the role of course, and I was given a small part in 6-10 episodes."[52]

About the same time as *Leave it to Beaver* began, Robert continued going on other auditions, acting in a few commercials, landing a

---

[51] Robert Mittelstaedt, emailed to author, September 12, 2014.

[52] Ibid.

movie role in *The Music Box Kid* (originally titled *The Gangster*), and getting a back-up role for a character in the traveling production of *Annie Get Your Gun*. Eventually, the calls for parts in *Leave it to Beaver* stopped coming and at age 16, when he would've had to join the Screen Actors' Guild and pay dues higher than what he was earning, Robert made the decision not to join.

After his stint on *Leave it to Beaver*, Robert never acted again. But he has no bitterness about the show or a lack of an acting career. He looks back at his time as an actor with good memories. "The best part was hanging around the set" (even though he did get in trouble once for being late to the director's call when he and Jerry were playing in Jerry's trailer.) He added that the best part of all was, "Going to the studio dining room and eating next to the stars." He also preferred his work in commercials and on *Leave it to Beaver* to the hard work his friends did delivering newspapers.

His time on *Leave it to Beaver* was also a great way to get in touch with old friends. Sometimes they would give him a call at his office at 2:00 p.m. and say, "I just saw you on *Leave it to Beaver*." He may have never said so out loud, but often wondered, "What were they doing watching TV at 1:30 in the afternoon?" His child and step-children have seen him in the show and he can't wait until he can show his granddaughter who at 18 months, is still a little too young to appreciate his acting chops on Beaver.

With acting no longer on his radar, Robert turned to education. He attended Claremont Men's College where he graduated magna cum laude and then attended the University of Virginia Law School, graduating in 1973. Before law school, Robert took time to join the Peace Corps and dreamed of spending his time in Nigeria, but war prevented that dream from coming true. Instead, he was sent to the middle of the Pacific Ocean to an atoll named Pulap in Micronesia. The island was home to 50 men in loincloth, 50 women in skirts, topless, and 100, for the most part, naked children. They had no electricity, no modern conveniences, but as Robert tells it, "They were the happiest, healthiest, most together people I'd ever known."[53]

---

[53] ibid

His next stop in the United States was law school, a place where he sported a Fu Manchu mustache, hair down to the middle of his back and he was known as someone who never wore sandals or shoes. Former FBI Director Mulller said at a UVA Law School speech years later, that Robert looked like a slacker who could care less about grades, but the man who would help hunt for Osama Bin Laden and become one of Robert's best friends, admitted Robert received some of the best grades in the class. [54]

His time in law school and his 40 years as an anti-trust lawyer (in 2008 he was given the "Attorney of the Year Award for Litigation")[55] have proven that his first appearance on *Leave it to Beaver*, as the smartest kid in the school in the episode, "Part-time Genius," was true to life. Today Robert is a partner for a well respected San Francisco law firm.

**Mustin, Burt** (1884-1977) Gus the Fireman

One of Beaver Cleaver's best friends on the show was not a classmate or next door neighbor, but a fireman named Gus who worked alone at auxiliary fire station #7. There must not have been mandatory retirement laws in Mayfield since the actor who portrayed Gus was 73 years old when *Leave it to Beaver* debuted. It's interesting to note that actor Burt Mustin did not even begin professional acting until he was 67 years old. Not that he didn't act before Hollywood, he certainly did.

Burt was a performer from the age of six when a drunk man heard him singing on his way home from kindergarten and took him into a saloon to sing. He stayed there all afternoon and evening and arrived home after dark. His pockets were full of money but his parents didn't care. He still received a stern punishment. In 1893, you can imagine what that punishment was, a big 'ole whippin'

[54] Robert S. Mueller, III, "Presentation of the Thomas Jefferson Foundation Medal in Law" (lecture, University of Virginia School of Law, Charlottesville, VA, April 12, 2013).

[55] "Robert A. Mittelstaedt," JonesDay.com, accessed September 9, 2014, http://www.jonesday.com/ramittelstaedt/.

from his dad. Burt was a singer, dancer and actor his entire life, but instead of hitting the road on the vaudeville circuit, he stayed put in Pittsburgh, working first as an engineer and then selling cars until 1941.[56]

In his first Hollywood role, Mustin played a marshal in *The Last Outpost* which starred Ronald Regan and featured Hugh Beaumont, the future Ward Cleaver. After his appearance in *The Last Outpost*, Burt Mustin was in great demand. He landed numerous roles in TV shows before *Leave it to Beaver*, these included, *The Adventures of Kit Carson*, *The Abbott and Costello Show*, *Schlitz Playhouse*, *The Loretta Young Show*, *Mayor of the Town*, *The Great Gildersleeve*, *Dragnet*, *Father Knows Best*, *Our Miss Brooks* and *The Lone Ranger*. The above are just some of 30+ TV shows in which he appeared in before *Leave it to Beaver*. By the time he became Beaver's friend, Burt Mustin was a very seasoned professional actor.[57] After *Leave it to Beaver*, Burt Mustin worked almost up to the day he died. His last TV role was on the show *Phyllis* in 1976 at the age of 92. He passed away only months later.

A testimonial on how he lived and prospered so long, Burt once told a friend the following when he was at the ripe old age of 80: "Don't drink, don't smoke, married to one girl for 54 years and never fooled around, watch my diet and exercise."[58] Sounds like a winning combination for everyone, doesn't it? Fireman Gus was a wealth of wisdom and now we know he lived out that wisdom himself.

## Osmond, Ken (b.1943) Eddie Haskell

Ken Osmond didn't have a typical childhood, but maybe it was more typical in the Hollywood area than some people might think. Instead of going outside to play ball with the fellas after school, Ken

---

[56] Cecil Smith, "For Burt Mustin, Life Begins at 87," *Toledo Blade*, June 5, 1971.

[57] "Burt Mustin" IMDB.com.

[58] Smith, "For Burt Mustin, Life Begins at 87."

and his brother Dayton were regularly ushered to auditions for commercials, TV shows and films by their mother. "It was what it was," Ken was recently heard saying when interviewed by Stu Shostak. While some childhood actors harbor bitterness toward their early career or toward those responsible for that career, like a parent, Ken has stated he has no bitterness at all because he enjoyed acting.[59]

In a 2006 interview, Ken told Bill O'Reilly, "Eddie has been good to me for almost fifty years now, has opened doors, and I've got to go places, and see things, and meet people, it's just unimaginable."[60] Ken has, over the years, imparted the same sort of accolades for *Leave it to Beaver* as the rest of the cast has done, "I am so proud to have been part of that show."[61]

But there was life before *Leave it to Beaver* for Ken Osmond. His acting career began in 1952, five years before *Leave it to Beaver*. His first role was in *Plymouth Adventure* (starring Spencer Tracy) as one of the kids crossing the Atlantic in the Mayflower. His brother Dayton was also a fellow shipmate in the film. He had a few more uncredited film roles under his belt before focusing on TV shows. In 1957 alone, he appeared in five television shows before his debut in *Leave it to Beaver* in November of that year. During the filming of *Leave it to Beaver*, Ken also appeared in one episode of each of the following shows, *Lassie*, *Wagon Train* and *Maverick*.

Like most actors from *Leave it to Beaver*, due to its popular success in syndication, Ken was typecast. For him, casting directors saw him only as Eddie Haskell, the smug, annoying teen who was quick with insincere flattery. While he did obtain a few roles after *Leave it to Beaver* in shows like *Lassie*, *The Munsters* and *Petticoat Junction*, Ken turned his pursuits elsewhere. His first venture was as owner

---

[59] "John N. Goudas, "From Eddie Haskell to the LAPD," *Chicago Tribune*, November 12, 1992, accessed September 23, 2014, http://articles.chicagotribune.com/1992-11-12/features/9204120704_1_beaver-motorcycle-cop-top-cops.

[60] Ken Osmond, interviewed by Bill O'Reilly, 2006.

[61] Ken Osmond, interviewed by Jamie Colby, 2007.

of a helicopter service with his brother which only lasted until 1966 after a helicopter crash.[62] Four years later, he entered the LAPD, barely passing the weight requirements, only doing so after drinking shakes and eating bananas for days before his physical. [63]

Ken worked as a motorcycle officer for the LAPD. One evening he chased after a stolen taxi and eventually wound up chasing after the thief on foot. He followed him down an alley, assuming he had kept running, but the suspect had stopped in the alley and pointed the gun and shot three times at the former *Leave it to Beaver* star. After being shot by the car thief, the thief walked toward him methodically and was about to put a final deadly bullet into Ken until his partner Henry Lane jumped the thief and scuffled with him. Both Ken and the thief were transported to the hospital in the same ambulance.[64]

After retiring from the LAPD, Ken returned to acting in the 1983 TV movie, *Still the Beaver*. He acted on the subsequent TV series, "*The New Leave it to Beaver*," in 101 episodes, which was four more appearances than he made in the original series. Both of Ken's sons, Christian and Eric, appeared with him in *The New Leave it to Beaver*.

Over all the years since the original show aired, Ken Osmond has grown more fond of the show. In one of his more recent interviews, he was asked if he ever watches episodes of *Leave it to Beaver*. "When they're on, sure, they're good shows." And asked if he ever sees scenes in which he'd change something, Ken answered, "I watch them as a viewer, not a participant. They're more enjoyable that way." [65]

Fellow cast member Barbara Billingsley said of Ken Osmond, "That man was so good in that role...He is a very nice man." She spoke of how well he acted because in real life, he was not the

---

[62] *People*, Where Are They Now?, March 04.1985, 97.

[63] Jerry Mathers interviewed by Gary Rutkowski.

[64] Goudas, "From Eddie Haskell to the LAPD."

[65] Ken Osmond, interviewed by LA TV Examiner, December, 2013, Hollywood, CA.

annoying pest he portrayed in the series. He basically was the only actor who had to be a totally different person than in real life. Billingsley also spoke of a time she accepted a dinner invite from Ken and his wife during the filming of *The New Leave it to Beaver*, "We sat down to have dinner and that awful Eddie Haskell, sitting at the end of the table said grace. Now that doesn't sound like Eddie, but nice man, nice family."[66]

The kindness of Barbara Billingsley has not been lost on Ken. At a reunion of *Leave it to Beaver* castmates for the release of the series on DVD, he mentioned in answer to a question about the Cleaver matriarch, who was too ill at the time to attend the release party, "My favorite person in the world is Barbara Billingsley."[67]

Jerry Mathers has expressed the same feelings about Ken and his acting ability, "… probably the best actor on the show…the reason I find Ken Osmond to be such a wonderful actor is the juxtaposition between Ken Osmond and Eddie Haskell." Mathers went on to describe Osmond's duties as a police officer for 18 years on the LAPD, his getting shot while chasing a car thief on foot down a dark alley and his dedication to the job. "That's nothing that Eddie Haskell would ever do, but that's the kind of person Ken Osmond is. I think he's the best actor on the show because he's so different [than his character]."[68]

### Bank, Frank (1942-2013) Lumpy Rutherford

If you own the season one DVD set of *Leave it to Beaver*, you've gone through all the bonus material and heard the Stu Show interview with Frank Bank and Jerry Mathers. It is an amazing interview and Frank Bank's fun loving personality brilliantly shines

---

[66] Barbara Billingsley interviewed by Karen Herman.

[67] "Adam Buckman, "Leave It to Beaver: Where Are They Now?," Xfinity.comcast.net, July 14, 2010, accessed September 17, 2014, http://xfinity.comcast.net/blogs/tv/2010/07/14/leave-it-to-beaver-where-are-they-now/.

[68] Jerry Mathers interviewed by Gary Rutkowski.

through in the mere 30 minutes of questions and answers. My fondness for Lumpy grew exponentially after hearing that interview. I was astonished that "Dumpy Lumpy" and Beaver had become friends along with becoming financial advisor/client. Frank tells some wonderful stories and also does so in his book, *Call Me Lumpy: My Leave it to Beaver Days and Other Wild Hollywood Life*.

One could say Frank Bank started off his Hollywood career with a splash. His first role, at age seven, was in the Broderick Crawford film, *Cargo to Capetown* (1950). Here is how his role is listed in IMDB, "Frank Bank: He got washed overboard in the first scene (uncredited)." From that humble beginning, no one could have suspected that Frank would one day stay in front of the public on the small screen, continuously, for almost 60 years, as he has done through *Leave it to Beaver* reruns.

Following his debut role which was almost over before the movie began, Frank appeared in three more TV shows before his audition for *Leave it to Beaver*, the most prominent of those was in *Father Knows Best*. Even after he earned the role of Lumpy Rutherford and while *Leave it to Beaver* was in production, Frank worked on the TV Movie *Life of Archie*, playing the title role opposite *Leave it to Beaver*'s Cheryl Holdridge who played Julie Foster, one of Wally's love interests. The TV movie was basically the pilot for a new *Life of Archie* TV series which never materialized, due in part to the sponsor seeing more Lumpy Rutherford in his performance than Archie Andrews. With that typecasting in place, Frank called it a career.

There is no denying the importance of Lumpy Rutherford to the show. He is one of the most loved characters, even though he was a bumbling oaf at times and really mean to Beaver on occasion, especially in "Beaver's Freckles." Fans will recognize the character of Lumpy Rutherford becoming more essential in storylines as Beaver Cleaver grew older and the focus of the show turned towards Wally. Here is a breakdown of how many episodes featured Frank Bank over the run of *Leave it to Beaver*; Season one (2); season two (8); season three (3); season four (8); season five (18); and season six (11).

After *Leave it to Beaver*, with the Archie series off the radar, Frank

Bank focused his future on business and investing. While other characters on the set of *Leave it to Beaver* read comic books during breaks in filming, he claims to have read the Wall Street Journal.[69] As Ken Osmond noted in the introduction of Frank's sometimes tawdry autobiography, "Frank has some working brain cells. They just don't show when you first meet him. I don't know why."[70] Before branching out into his own career in business, he and his brother worked in their parent's thriving meat market.[71]

Frank went on to make quite a living as a licensed financial advisor who dealt mostly in tax-free municipal bonds. Among his notable clients were fellow *Leave it to Beaver* actors Barbara Billingsley and Jerry Mathers. He did venture back onto the small screen when the entire gang filmed *Still the Beaver* in 1983 and he co-starred in *The New Leave it to Beaver* from 1984-1989. He often talked fondly of his time on *Leave it to Beaver* in interviews and at cast reunions up until his death in 2013, one day after celebrating his 71st birthday…R.I.P Lumpy.

### Beaird, Pamela (b. 1945) Mary Ellen Rogers

The actress who played the love of Wally's life, only appeared in five *Leave it to Beaver* episodes as Mary Ellen Rogers. They were "My Brother's Girl," "Dance Contest," "Wally, the Lifeguard," "Wally and Dudley," and "Wally's Weekend Job." She also played the character Myra in "Wally's Orchid."

While Pamela Baird only appeared in a total of six episodes, five as Mary Ellen Rogers, her name was heard spoken by either Wally, his friends, or his parents in numerous other episodes. Her last acting credit occurred in 1964 as she played "the third girl" in the *Perry Mason* episode, "The Case of the Careless Kidnapper."

---

[69] Nick Charles, "Forever Lumpy," *People*, May 04, 1998.

[70] Elaine Woo, "Frank Bank Dies at 71; Played 'Lumpy' on 'Leave It to Beaver'," *Los Angeles Times*, April 15, 2013, accessed September 17, 2014, http://articles.latimes.com/2013/apr/15/local/la-me-frank-bank-20130416.

[71] Charles, "Forever Lumpy."

She has moved on in life to become a music and drama teacher, having earned a masters degree in education and was last reported to be working on a doctorate degree. She has also been blessed with a great marriage and five wonderful children. [72] Pamela did not reprise her role as Mary Ellen Rogers on *The New Leave it to Beaver*. That role was played by actress Janice Kent.

## Fafara, Tiger (b.1945)  Tooey Brown

The actor who played one of Wally Cleaver's best friends grew up around Hollywood, spending most of his youth in Studio City. Tiger Fafara was one of many child actors whose acting desire was prodded along by a very enthusiastic mother. At a young age, both Tiger and his younger brother Stanley, who portrayed Whitey Whitney on *Leave it to Beaver*, were chauffeured by their mother to auditions all over Hollywood for TV commercials and TV shows in the early 1950s.

Tiger was quite active in the years before his *Leave it to Beaver* audition and subsequent role as Tooey Brown. He had acted in 16 TV shows and 2 movies from 1953 to 1957. He also had numerous commercials under his belt. A few of his acting credits included, *I Led 3 Lives*, *My Friend Flicka*, *Lassie* and *Make Room for Daddy*.

In 1956 or early 1957, their mother took both boys to an open casting call for *Leave it to Beaver*. After their auditions, Tiger secured the role of Wally's friend Tooey while his younger brother was offered the part of Whitey Whitney. Tiger acted in 18 episodes of *Leave it to Beaver* through the first three seasons. He appeared in eight episodes in season one, eight episodes in season two, and only "Wally's Election" and "Wally, the Businessman," in season three. This was in stark contrast to his brother Stanley who worked on the show all six seasons.

After *Leave it to Beaver*, Tiger acted in only one other show, *My Three Sons*, before taking a 20 year absence from the small screen. He later returned in *Still the Beaver*, a 1983 TV reunion movie and he

---

[72] "Inthebeginning.com/pamelabeaird.htm," Inthebeginning.com, accessed October 1, 2014, http://www.inthebeginning.com/PamelaBeaird.htm.

appeared in two episodes of *The New Leave it to Beaver* series. After 1987, there is no record of him acting again.

Tiger made a great contribution to the early seasons of *Leave it to Beaver*. He's known to an entire generation as Tooey Brown but to a newer, younger generation, a hard rockin' generation, he is better known by rock n' roll fans as the father of the talented Dez Fafara, lead singer of metal bands DevilDriver and Coal Chamber.

## Hart, Buddy (b.1944) Chester Anderson

Chester Anderson was played by the son of a very famous TV character, the Lone Ranger. Buddy Hart's father John played the masked man in 1952-1953 while Clayton Moore was embroiled in some nasty contract negotiations with the producers of *The Lone Ranger*.

His acting basically started with *Leave it to Beaver* in 1957. About that same time, he also appeared in the *Schlitz Playhouse* and in the film, *Outlaw's Son*. His work in television after *Leave it to Beaver* was sparse. He appeared on one episode of *My Three Sons* in 1961, a *Twilight Zone* episode in 1962, an episode of the *Donna Reed Show* in 1963 and his final TV appearance was in 1965 on *Wagon Train*. He continued on with bit parts in the movies *Ice Station Zebra*, *Changes* (one of the best independent films to portray life in the late 1960s), and *Sweet Charity* in 1969.

Hart's Chester Anderson was not a major character in any *Leave it to Beaver* episodes, but Hart played the part well. He was one of the first friends of Wally we get to meet. He first appeared in the sixth episode of season one in, "Brotherly Love." He holds a fond place in the heart of many *Leave it to Beaver* fans and I apologize there is not more information I can share with you about Buddy Hart.

# Other Recurring Characters

## Deacon, Richard (1921-1984) Fred Rutherford

The role of Fred Rutherford is one of only two parents of any significance on *Leave it to Beaver* other than Ward and June Cleaver, the other being Larry's mom, Mrs. Mondello. While Richard Deacon only appeared 23 times over the six years of the show, he, like quite a few *Beaver* characters, is referred to in many other episodes.

During 1960-1961 (season 4) he only appeared in two episodes of *Leave it to Beaver*. But during this same time period he stayed quite busy with other work, appearing in 25 different television shows in addition to his *Leave it to Beaver* work. Some of those TV shows included *The Untouchables, Bonanza, Make Room for Daddy, The Rifleman, My Three Sons, Perry Mason, The Jack Benny Program, The Adventures of Ozzie and Harriet, The Donna Reed Show* and *Mister Ed*. Richard Deacon kept himself very busy and one can only imagine that if he had not been such a successful actor, he may have had even more appearances on *Leave it to Beaver*.

Before his role as Fred Rutherford came to an end, Richard Deacon had a larger recurring role on prime time, that of Mel Cooley on *The Dick Van Dyke Show*. It's hard to imagine an actor having two recurring roles on television shows at the same time, especially during an era when there were only three networks, but that's exactly what happened to the man who played an irritating oaf in Mayfield and a bumbling example of nepotism in New York as the producer of the Alan Brady Show.

The TV shows he worked on after *Leave it to Beaver* is simply too long to list. Suffice it to say, he played on the best the 60s and 70s had to offer. He also appeared in the Broadway production of *Hello Dolly*, playing the part of Horace Vandergelder. He worked right up to his death in 1984, finishing his career with 180 acting credits.

Richard Deacon stayed busy his entire life, whether in film, TV, Broadway or in the kitchen. Most fans may not know he was a gourmet chef and even hosted a Canadian TV program on microwave cooking in the 1970s. He also wrote a cookbook about the subject.[73] So at the Rutherford house, it wasn't his wife Gwen doing all the cooking, the family sometimes had to wait for him to return from the "old salt mine" before they could eat.

**Packer, Doris** (1904-1979) Principal Cornelia Rayburn

Appearing in 17 different episodes of *Leave it to Beaver*, Packer had her biggest influence in the first and sixth seasons of the show. Born in Menominee, Michigan, it didn't take long for her family to move to warmer climates after her birth. She spent her formative years in Los Angles where she caught the acting bug during high school, participating in many school productions. She later attended UCLA and after college moved to New York City to study acting.[74]

While in New York City, during the 1930s, Packer performed in numerous Broadway plays. She later married stage director Roland G. Edwards, although 25 years his junior, proof that love has no age boundaries. When not performing in Broadway shows, Packer also performed on radio. Among the shows she was heard in were *The Aldrich Family* and *Mr. & Mrs. North*.[75]

During World War II, Packer enlisted in the Women Army Corps. She entered the army as a private and mustered out as a Sergeant. After the war, she continued living in New York City until the early 1950s when she moved to Glendale, CA, possibly in 1952 or early 1953. Her husband passed away soon after their move out west.

While Doris Packer may be best known, at least to *Leave it to Beaver* fans, as the very proper, authority figure Principal Cornelia Rayburn, she also had very successful runs on other TV Shows during the 1950s and 1960s. She appeared in nine episodes of the

---

[73] "Richard Deacon," IMDB.com, accessed September 29, 2014, http://www.imdb.com/name/nm0212586/.

[74] *Wikipedia contributors.* "Doris Packer," accessed September 29, 2014, http://en.wikipedia.org/w/index.php?title=Doris_Packer&oldid=625373590.

[75] "Doris Packer," IMDB.com, accessed September 29, 2014, http://www.imdb.com/name/nm0655481/.

*George Burns and Gracie Allen Show* as Mrs. Sohmers along with seven other characters in seven earlier episodes. She played Clarice Osborn in *The Many Lives of Dobie Gillis* from 1960 to 1963. She played this role while simultaneously appearing in *Leave it to Beaver*.

Other TV shows in which she had multiple or recurring roles were *The Jack Benny Program*, *Happy*, *Lux Video Theater*, *The Bob Cummings Show*, *It's a Great Life*, *The Beverly Hillbillies* and *The New Dick Van Dyke Show*.

Doris Packer's last appearance came in the 1975 film *Shampoo* as Rozalind. The movie starred Warren Beatty, Julie Christie and Goldie Hawn.

# Remaining season one actors in alphabetical order

**Alden, Norman** (1924 - 2012) "Water Anyone" (Water Dept. Worker)

During his first year acting in TV, Norman Alden played a bit role on the 7th episode of *Leave it to Beaver*, "Water Anyone?" He plays a water department worker who tells Beaver that the water will be shut off for the afternoon. After *Leave it to Beaver*, Alden went on to become a prolific character actor. Internet Movie Database mentions he acted or did voice over work in 2,500 movies, TV shows and commercials.

**Allen, Gary** (b. 1942) "Beaver Gets 'Spelled'" (First Man); "Larry's Club" (Boy in Club)

Gary Allen's best known works were small parts in *Annie Hall*, *Mommie Dearest* and *The Hudsucker Proxy*. He worked continually from 1975 through 1986 in many TV shows and films although he began his career on *The Jack Benny Program* in 1956. He worked sparingly in the 1950s and 1960s.

**Allen, Ricky** (b. 1945?) "The Train Trip" (Boy in station)

As with many *Leave it to Beaver* actors, Ricky Allen also made an appearance on *Lassie*. He made one appearance on *Leave it to Beaver* as "Boy in station" on the episode "The Train Trip." His biggest acting success came as Sudsy Pfeiffer on *My Three Sons* from 1961-1963. In 1967 and 1969 he made his final two television appearances, these were on *My Three Sons* as the characters "Hoby" and "Larry" respectively.

# B

**Bacon, Irving** (1893 - 1965) "Captain Jack" (Postal clerk)

Irving Bacon is one of the most prolific of the character actors who appeared in *Leave it to Beaver*. He debuted in a silent short in 1915 and his final screen appearance was on The Dick Van Dyke Show in 1965. But 538 of his 540 credits were filmed in only a 37 year span from 1923-1960. That averages over 14 films or TV shows each year. Amazingly, he only played one part on *Leave it to Beaver* in all those many roles. He played the postal clerk who handed Wally and Beaver their pet alligator in a very small box on the episode "Captain Jack."

**Baker, Benny** (1907-1994) "The Haircut" (Barber)

 On the fourth episode of *Leave it to Beaver*, "The Haircut," Beaver tries convincing a barber to cut his hair even though he "losted" his money, Benny Baker was this barber. This was his only *Leave it to Beaver* appearance out of his 133 acting credits.  He began his career in vaudeville in the 1920s and eventually wound up working in film from the 1930s through the 1940s. Beginning in 1952, Benny Baker had regular work in television, his livelihood, with an occasional foray onto the big screen as he did in *Boy, Did I Get a Wrong Number* with Bob Hope and *Paint Your Wagon* starring Lee Marvin and Clint Eastwood.

**Bennett, Julie** (b. 1929) "The Black Eye" (Waitress)

Well known for her work in animated shorts and features such as *Spider Man*, *Yogi Bear* and *The Bugs Bunny & Tweety Show*, Julie made her only appearance on *Leave it to Beaver* as a waitress in "The Black Eye." She was also a co-writer on Woody Allen's debut film *What's Up Tiger Lilly?*

**Berwald,Tommy** (b. 1945) "The Black Eye" (Third boy)

The Hollywood career of Tommy Berwald began and ended with his playing the third boy in "The Black Eye."

**Best, Dorothy** (b. 1948) "Party Invitation" (First girl at the party)

Now a producer, Dorothy Best made her acting debut on *Leave it to Beaver* in "Party Invitation," as the First Girl at the Party. She has been married to James Best (Roscoe P. Coltrane from Dukes of Hazzard) since 1986.

**Bremen, Leonard** (1915 - 1986) "It's a Small World/Pilot" (Milk Bar Proprietor)

Appearing in uncredited roles, Leonard Bremen had parts in many big movies of the mid-1940s such as *Dark Passage* starring Humphrey Bogart, *Deep Valley* with Ida Lupino, *Buck Privates Come Home* with Abbot & Costello and *It Happened in Brooklyn* with Frank Sinatra. He finished out his career with bit parts in comedies like *The Beverly Hillbillies*, *The Brady Bunch* and *Different Strokes*.

**Brewster, Diane**  (1931-1991) "It's a Small World" (Miss Simms); "Beaver Gets 'Spelled'" (Miss Canfield); "Beaver's Crush" (Miss Canfield); "Part-time Genius" (Miss Canfield); and "Beaver and Poncho" (Miss Canfield).

Diane Brewster first appeared in the *Leave it to Beaver* television pilot tilted "It's a Small World," in the role of Miss Simms, a secretary. She was one talented woman who had a busy career before *Leave it to Beaver* was on her radar, beginning TV work when she was 24 years old. During and after *Leave it to Beaver*, Diane Brewster also had roles on many westerns such as *Cheyenne*, *Wagon Train*, *Death Valley Days* and *Maverick*. She was one of the original cast who filmed the *Still the Beaver* movie in 1983 and she also appeared in four episodes of *The New Leave it to Beaver*. It is hard to believe Diane Brewster only appeared in four episodes of Leave it to Beaver. She passed away of heart failure in Studio City, CA in 1991.

**Bryar, Claudia** (1918-2011) "Party Invitation" (Mrs. Dennison); "Beaver's Library Book," (Librarian); "Community Chest" (Mrs. Harris); "Three Boys and a Burro" (Mrs. Bates)

In addition to *Leave it to Beaver*, there were four other TV shows in which Claudia Bryar played multiple roles. These shows included *The F.B.I.*, *Wagon Train*, *Bonanza* and *Barnaby Jones*. She also had small roles in movies such as *Pat Garrett and Billy the Kid*, *Psycho II* and *Bad Company* with Jeff Bridges. Claudia even had an uncredited role as a beauty operator in the film *Giant*.

**Buchanan, Edgar** (1903-1979) "Captain Jack" (Captain Jack); "Uncle Billy" (Uncle Billy/William Cleaver"); "Uncle Billy's Visit" (Uncle Billy/William Cleaver)

Better known to *Leave it to Beaver* fans for his portrayal of Uncle Billy, Edgar Buchanan was first seen on the show in the episode titled, "Captain Jack. His two other appearances were in "Uncle Billy," and "Uncle Billy's Visit." His first big role on TV was as Sheriff Red Connors on *Hopalong Cassidy*. He made forty appearances on *Hopalong*. Buchanan is best known for his role on *Petticoat Junction* as Uncle Joe Carson, a character he also portrayed on *Green Acres* and *The Beverly Hillbillies*. Before acting, Buchanan was a dentist for many years in Eugene, Oregon. He met his wife while attending dental school and was married for fifty years to wife Mildred. Edgar Buchanan passed away in 1979 from a stroke, ten days before his 51st anniversary.

**Budzak, Betty Lynn** (b. 1947) "Party Invitation" (2nd girl at the party"); "Beaver's Poster" (Student); "The Dramatic Club" (Victoria Bennett).

Betty Lynn Budzak appeared on three episodes of *Leave it to Beaver*. In her final appearance, she played opposite Beaver in a school play where the two have to kiss. After her three appearances on *Leave it to Beaver*, Betty Lynn Budzak never again had a film or TV role. Could she have been related to a cameraman or some other studio staff member? We'd all like to know what happened to Betty Lynn.

# C

**Carpenter, Penny** (b. 1945) "Captain Jack" (Girl to see Captain Jack)

The pinnacle of Penny Carpenter's Hollywood career was her role as a girl to see Captain Jack in the episode "Captain Jack." Before *Leave it to Beaver*, she did have uncredited roles in *The Harder They Fall* starring Humphrey Bogart and *Gun For a Coward* starring Fred MacMurray, but nothing after *Leave it to Beaver*.

**Caroll, Cindy a.k.a. Cindy Sydes** (b. 1944) "Wally's Girl Trouble" (Penny Jamison); "Wally's Test," (Nita Norton); "Wally's Election," (Alma Hanson); "School Sweater" (Helen); "Wally and Alma" (Alma Hanson); "Wally, the Lifeguard," (Alma Hanson); and "Eddie's Double-Cross" (Alma Hanson).

Only 22 actors on *Leave it to Beaver* had more appearances on the show than Cindy Carol. She appeared in 7 episodes, playing three different characters. After her stint on *Leave it to Beaver* ended in 1960, she later found success on *The New Loretta Young Show* in the role of Binkie Massey (26 episodes) and later played Susan in the soap opera *Never Too Young* (20 episodes). Tony Dow also appeared in a recurring role on *Never Too Young*.

**Carroll, Virginia** (1913-2009) "It's a Small World" (Nurse)

After co-starring in numerous "B" westerns, Virginia Carroll tried her hand at television beginning in the 1950s. She had bit parts on such shows as *The Adventures of Superman*, *Fireside Theater* and *The Adventures of Kit Carson* before her appearance on the *Leave it to Beaver* pilot, "It's a Small World" in 1957. Virginia Carroll appeared most often on *The Roy Rogers Show* (5 episodes) and *Dragnet* (4 episodes).

**Coates,Phyllis** (b. 1927) "New Neighbors" (Betty Donaldson)

You have heard of stars being discovered at the corner of Hollywood and Vine, here is one example. Phyllis Coates was discovered by comedian Ken Murray in a restaurant on that famous corner after her move from Wichita Falls, Texas. She began working in his Vaudeville show and the rest is history. In 1957 she played the role of Betty Donaldson in the episode "New Neighbors." At the time, she was married to *Leave it to Beaver* director Norman Tokar.

**Corby, Ellen** (1911-1999) "Lonesome Beaver" (Pedestrian)

From 1933 to 1947 she had uncredited roles in many films before playing Aunt Trina in the 1948 film *I Remember Mama*. However, she is best known for her role as Grandma on *The Walton's*. She was a pedestrian in "Lonesome Beaver," the only episode of *Leave it to Beaver* in which she appeared.

**Crehan, Joseph** (1883 - 1966) "Train Trip" (Train Conductor)

Appearing in his first film in 1916, Crehan eventually worked in almost 400 films and television shows. He played the role of the train conductor on the "Train Trip" episode. He had moderate success in the early 60s with regular work on *The Untouchables* and *The Andy Griffith Show*.

**Curtis, Barry** (b. 1943) "Boarding School" (Johnny Franklin); "Wally and Alma" (Harry Myers)

Before appearing on *Leave it to Beaver* episodes "Boarding School," and "Wally and Alma," Barry Curtis had a starring role in *The Adventures of Champion* as Ricky North. He retired from his acting career after his final appearance in *Leave it to Beaver*.

# D

**Davis, Charles** (1925-2009) "Part-Time Genius" and "The Broken Window" (Corny Cornelius)

Playing many bit parts in film and on TV in the 1950s, Charles Davis found regular work in the late 1950s and early 60s in shows such as *Perry Mason, Alfred Hitchcock Presents* and *The Wild Wild West*. He closed out his career in the mid-1980s with small roles on some of the best prime time shows like *Remington Steele, L.A. Law, Dynasty, Falcon Crest, Murder She Wrote and Highway to Heaven*.

**De Sales, Francis** (1912-1988) "Water Anyone?" (Mr. Anderson)

De Sales was best known for his role on the series *Mr. & Mrs. North* as Lt. Weingand. He found regular work after *Leave it to Beaver* on *The Adventures of Ozzie and Harriet* and in a recurring role as Sheriff Maddox on *Two Faces West*.

**des Enfants, Gabrielle** (b. 1953) "Child Care" (Helen "Puddin'" Wilson)

A cute child actor, Gabrielle guest starred on "Child Care" in season one of *Leave it to Beaver*. She also appeared in three other television shows, *Tales of Wells Fargo, Wagon Train* and *McHale's Navy*.
**Dodd, Barbara** (b. 1930) "Wally's Girl Trouble" (Librarian)

When Wally in "Wally's Girl Trouble" goes to the library for Penny Jamison, he asks the librarian, played by Barbara Dodd where he could find *Rebecca of Sunnybrook Farm*. This was Barbara's only appearance on *Leave it to Beaver* and she later went behind the scenes in Hollywood to work as a casting director while still accepting occasional TV roles. Her latest was as Ellen on *Modern Family* in the episode, "Me? Jealous?" in 2012.

**Doran, Ann** (1911-2000) "Voodoo Magic" (Agnes Haskell); "Beaver the Magician" (Mrs. Bellamy)

Ann Doran was a prolific character actor and some accounts have her working in over 1500 movies and television shows. However, IMDB only lists her with officially 366 acting credits to her name. Her first film was Douglas Fairbanks' silent *Robin Hood* in 1922.

**Dore, Anne** (b. 1930) "The Perfume Salesman" (Mrs. Wentworth)

Her most regular work in the 1950s was on *The Red Skelton Hour* and *Space Patrol*. Her last Hollywood role was as a female giant in *Land of the Giants* (1968).

# E

**Engle, Paul** (b. 1948) "Wally's Girl Trouble" (Second boy in library); "Beaver's Bike" (Bicycle thief)

Regular work in Hollywood was no stranger to Paul Engle. His career spanned from 1955-1962 and during that time he amassed forty acting credits, most of those in television. His last TV show was *Hazel* in 1962.

# F

**Fawcett, William** (1894-1974) "Beaver's Crush" (Mr. Johnson)

In "Beaver's Crush," William Fawcett plays the character of Mr. Johnson in one of his almost 400 television and film roles. Before acting, Fawcett was a professor at Michigan State University teaching theater arts. He played in numerous television productions in which he appeared in six or seven episodes, such as *The Cisco Kid, Wagon Train, The Virginian, Gunsmoke, Bonanza* among many others, but his most regular role was as Clayton in *Duffy's Tavern* in 1954.

**Flowers, Bess** (1898-1984) "Train Trip" (Lady in train station waiting room); "Beaver's Monkey" (June's luncheon guest )

In *Leave it to Beaver*, Bess Flowers made two uncredited appearances, the first in "Train Trip" and the second in "Beaver's Monkey." The Internet Movie Database has her listed officially as acting in 847 TV shows and movies, most of those as uncredited townspeople, lunch guests, diners or department store customers.

**Foran, Mary** (1919-1981) "Train Trip" (Lady hitting her little boy in train station)

With small roles in popular sitcoms in the 1960s, Mary Foran stayed busy in Hollywood helping people smile. The shows she appeared on are icons of American comedy, shows such as *Gilligan's Island, The Lucy Show, Mr. Ed, That Girl, The Monkees, I Dream of Jeannie* and *Bewitched*.

**Frye, Gil** (1918-2000) "The Paper Route" (Newspaper customer); "The Hair Cut" (Barber shop customer)

From 1942 to 1950, Gil Frye worked on numerous "B" movies in small roles. At the onset of the television era, he worked continuously through 1965, making his last appearance almost 20 years later on *Vega$* as a medical examiner. The television series in which he found the most work was *Perry Mason* where he played 10 roles from 1958-1965.

# G

**Gilchrist, Connie** (1901-1985) "Captain Jack" (Maid)

Playing a maid in the first ever filmed *Leave it to Beaver* episode, "Captian Jack," she refuses to clean the boy's bathroom if they're going to keep an alligator in there. Without knowing it, she blew the whistle on the boy's secret pet. Her longest running role was as Purity Pinker on the series, *The Adventures of Long John Silver*.

**Gillum, Jan** (b. 1945) "My Brother's Girl" (Jan Gillum)

In "My Brother's Girl," Jan Gillum plays Kathleen who is sitting at a lunchroom table with Mary Ellen Rogers. She also played 12 year old Yolanda in the movie *Somebody Up There Likes Me* starring Paul Newman, but after 1958, she has no other acting credits.

**Gleason, James** (1882-1959) "The Clubhouse" (Pete)

By two years, James Gleason was the oldest actor to appear on the first season of *Leave it to Beaver*. Burt Mustin (Gus the Fireman) was two years his junior. The role he played on his only *Leave it to Beaver* episode, "The Clubhouse," was that of Pete, a dishonest tramp who talks Beaver into donating him his hard earned money. In a very odd circumstance, James Gleason's last role ever was in the movie, *The Last Hurrah*, starring Spencer Tracy.

**Graham, Tim** (1904 - 1979) "It's a Small World" (Doc)

Born in Kansas, Tim Graham moved to Hollywood and began his career late in life, in his late 40s. He had bit parts and uncredited roles in the late 1940s and the 1950s before playing "Doc" on the *Leave it to Beaver* pilot, these included two times playing uncredited roles in Francis the Talking Mule films. He may be the only actor to ever appear in a film with a talking mule and a TV show with a talking beaver.

**Gray, Charles H.** (1921-2008) "New Neighbors" (Mr. Donaldson)

As Beaver's neighbor Mr. Donaldson, Charles Gray terrified Beaver in the episode, "New Neighbors." This was his only appearance on *Leave it to Beaver*. He is best known for his work on the western *Rawhide*, where he appeared on 30 episodes as cowboy Clay Forrester.

**Grayson, Phillip** (b. 1945) "The Black Eye" (First boy)

Appearing In only one *Leave it to Beaver* episode, "The Black Eye," Philip Grayson acted in an additional five television shows between 1957-1961. Finally retiring from the screen after a 1971 episode of *Hawaii Five-O*.

# H

**Halper, David** (1947-2005) "Beaver's Old Friend" (Friend #2)

In "Beaver's Old Friend," David Halper played one of the friends who were going out looking for pop bottles. Before heading out, they stop at Beaver's house and tease him because he's holding an old Teddy Bear Beaver has rescued from the trash. Halper did not stick with acting as his last known part was as Tommy Platt in a 1961 episode of *Bat Masterson*.

**Hammer, Stephen** (b. 1944?) "Wally's Girl Trouble" (Third boy in library)

In the episode, "Wally's Girl Trouble," Hammer plays a boy in the library giggling because Wally has come looking for a copy of *Rebecca of Sunnybrook Farm*. He only had a few roles in the late 50s and early 60s, his last being Roger on *The Donna Reed Show* in 1962.

**Hart, John** (1917-2009) "Lonesome Beaver" (Scoutmaster); "Beaver Plays Hooky" (Construction worker) "A Night in the Woods" (Forest Ranger)

The real life father of Wally's friend Chester Anderson, John Hart appeared in three episodes of *Leave it to Beaver*. His first two episodes were while his son played the role of Chester, they were, "Lonesome Beaver," in which he played the scoutmaster and "Beaver Plays Hooky," as a construction worker. His later role was as the forest ranger in "A Night in the Woods." John Hart is probably best known for his work as the Lone Ranger, replacing Clayton Moore in 1952 after a salary dispute.

**Hatton, Raymond** (1887-1971) "The Clubhouse" (Pete the Fireman)

It's almost unreal to think about an actor entering the movie business in 1909, but that's what Pete the Fireman from *Leave it to Beaver* did. He was only in one episode of *Leave it to Beaver*, "The Clubhouse," but his character of Pete the Fireman also appeared with a different actor in the episode, "Child Care." Hatton appeared in approximately 300 silent films and "B" movies from 1909-1950 before turning to the new medium of television. His last appearance was in the film, *In Cold Blood*.

**Holmes, Dennis** (b. 1950) "Beaver's Old Friend" (Friend #1)

In "Beaver's Old Friend," Dennis Holmes is the friend who leads a couple other boys in making fun of Beaver for playing with dolls. In this case, the doll was a Teddy Bear Beaver had rescued from the garbage can. Holmes continued acting until 1964 and is best known for his role as Mike Williams in the TV western, *Laramie*.

**Holmes, Wendell** (1914-1962) "Music Lesson" (T.J. Willet); "Beaver's Hero" (T.J. Willet); "Beaver and Andy" (Andy); "Beaver's English Test" (Mr. Blair); "Farewell to Penny" (Mr. Blair)
This is one of the few character actors on *Leave it to Beaver* who had a long career but found his most regular work with the Beav. He appeared in a total of five episodes. He died in Paris France of a heart attack not long after finishing his last episode on *Leave it to Beaver*.

**Hoyt, John** (1905-1991) "Part-Time Genius" (Dr. Compton); "Wally's New Suit" (Clothier); "Beaver's Accordion" (Mr. Franklin)

A very talented actor, John Hoyt had parts in some very good movies such as *Blackboard Jungle* and *Spartacus*. He also has a distinction among character actors, at least of all those in season one of *Leave it to Beaver*, of playing multiple roles (at least two) on most of the television shows on which he worked. In *Leave it to Beaver*, Hoyt's roles were Dr. Compton in "Part-Time Genius," the clothier in "Wally's New Suit," and Mr. Franklin from the accordion company in "Beaver's Accordion." He had a resurgence in his career in the 1980s when he was tapped to play Grandpa Stanley Kanisky for 78 episodes on *Gimme a Break*."

**Hunt, William** (??-??) "The Broken Window" (Grocer)

Hunt played a grocer in "The Broken Window," his only *Leave it to Beaver* episode. After *Leave it to Beaver*, he had a few roles in the 1960s and from 1964 to 1976 was absent from the small screen before returning to CBS for one shot roles in *One Day at a Time* and *All in the Family* in 1977.

# I  n/a

# J

**Jay, Helen** (1925-1989) "The Perfume Salesmen" (Perfume customer); "The Grass is Always Greener" (Woman)
After playing many uncredited and bit roles in "B" movies, including a few sci-fi films such as *The Space Children*, *She Devil* and *Space Master X-7*, Jay Helen made it to the set of *Leave it to Beaver* in "The Perfume Salesmen," and "The Grass is Always Greener." Her regular work in Hollywood ended in 1965 with an appearance in the film *Looking for Love* starring Connie Francis.

# K

**Karr, Raymond** (b. 1946) "My Brother's Girl" (Boy)

Karr only appeared in two television shows in a short lived career. He was possibly a friend or relative of a crew member. He appeared in "My Brother's Girl" credited as "boy." His only other TV show appearance was in *The Real McCoys* a year after Beaver.

**Kearns, Joseph** (1907-1962) "It's a Small World" (Mr. Crowley)

Playing the role of Mr. Crowley in the pilot episode "It's a Small World," Kearns did not appear in any *Leave it to Beaver* episodes that aired on television. He worked on many 1950s television shows including *The Burns and Allen Show*, *The Jack Benny Program*, *Our Miss Brooks*, *Gunsmoke* and is best known for his work as Mr. Wilson on *Dennis the Menace*. He was also a well know Old Time Radio actor, best known for his work on *Sherlock Holmes*. He also appeared along with Barbara Billingsley on the short lived TV series, *Professional Father* in 1955. Joseph Kearns died of a cerebral hemorrhage in Los Angeles on February 17, 1962.

**Kelk, Jackie** (1923-2002) "The Paper Route" (Old Man Merkel)

Who could forget Old Man Merkel? He was the boy's boss in the episode, "The Paper Route." Jackie Kelk had moderate success on TV. However, he was a great radio actor and for years, portrayed Henry Aldrich's best friend Homer Brown on *The Aldrich Family*. He also portrayed Homer Brown for the first two seasons on television. After *Leave it to Beaver*, his last two TV appearances were on *Bachelor Father* and *The Donna Reed Show*. He passed away in Rancho Mirage, CA in 2002.

**Kellogg, Ray** (1919-1981) "Cat Out of the Bag" (Mr. Donaldson); "Beaver's Old Buddy" (Mr. Waters)

Best known for two shows on which he worked quite regularly, *The Life and Legend of Wyatt Earp* and *The Red Skelton Comedy Hour*, Ray Kellogg also appeared on two *Leave it to Beaver* episodes. He played Mr. Donaldson in "Cat Out of the Bag," the last episode in season one where he replaced Charles H. Gray who originally played Mr. Donaldson earlier in the season. Later in the series, he played Mr. Waters in "Beaver's Old Buddy."

**Kendis, William** (1916-1980) "The State Versus Beaver" (Charlie - Police Officer)

How could anyone give a traffic ticket to sweet, little, adorable Beaver Cleaver? It was easy for William Kendis in his role as police officer Charlie in the episode "The State vs. Beaver." Kendis broke into television with a bang, making his debut on the crime drama Dragnet in 1956. He worked steadily until 1961 with appearances in *The Twilight Zone*, *The Rifleman*, *Perry Mason* and many other shows. His complete absence from the small screen occurred after his last role as Owens in *The Flying Nun* in 1967.

**Kennedy, Madge** (1891-1987) "Beaver's Short Pants" "Train Trip" "The Visiting Aunts" "Beaver the Magician" "Beaver's Prep School" (Aunt Martha)

Unlike a lot of actors with guest appearances on *Leave it to Beaver*, the woman lovingly known (at least by her niece June Cleaver) as Aunt Martha, had a long career (59 years) but did not wind up with hundreds of small roles. Instead, her total output was much less but was filled with decent to good roles, not uncredited walk on roles so many character actors must take to put food on the table. Some of the movies and TV shows she worked on were: *Lust for Life* starring Kirk Douglas, *Houseboat* starring Cary Grant, *They Shoot Horses, Don't They?* starring Jane Fonda, and *Alfred Hitchcock Presents*. Maybe her obtaining good roles had something to do with her years of success on Broadway beginning in 1912. In *Leave it to Beaver*, she guest starred in only five episodes, but was spoken of in many more.

**Kirkpatrick, Jess(e)** (1897-1976)

"Beaver's Old Friend" (Garbage Man) "The Grass is Always Greener" (Henry Fletcher) "Beaver Finds a Wallet" (Police Sergeant) "Chuckie's New Shoes" (Salesman) "The Big Fish Count" (Mr. Parker) "Wally Buys a Car" (Mr. Nelson)

If only Jess Kirkpatrick had been in a *Leave it to Beaver* episode in season 5, he would've been on the show at least once in every season. His final television appearance, out of his total of 169, was on *Mayberry R.F.D.* in 1969.

# L

**Lee, Joanna** (1931-2003) "My Brother's Girl" (librarian)

From 1956 to 1961, Joanna Lee was an aspiring actress. Beginning in 1961, she tried her hand at the other side of the TV camera and became a writer. She concentrated her efforts on animated fare when she began, writing shows for *Top Cat*, *The Jetsons* , *Mr. Magoo* and *The Flintstones* in the first half of the 1960s. She later wrote for numerous situation comedies and primetime dramas. She won a Primetime Emmy for her writing on *The Waltons'* "The Thanksgiving Story" episode.

**Lewis, Louise** (1914-1996) "Wally's Girl Trouble (Miss Higgins)

A very talented character actor who had her best success in the early 1970s drama *Medical Center*, Louise Lewis (Fitch) made only one appearance on the original *Leave it to Beaver* series. Lewis also holds the distinction of being only one of three actors from season one to appear in *The New Leave it to Beaver* who did not have a recurring role in the original Beaver series, the others being William Schallert and Lyle Talbot.

**Lowell, Linda** (b. 1945) "My Brother's Girl" (Frances).

In *There's No Business Like Show Business*, Linda Lowell played 8 year old Katy (the adult Katy was played by Mitzi Gaynor). Working in the same film as Ethel Merman and Marylin Monroe must have been exciting for Lowell and especially for her parents. The future was bright as this was only her third role in Hollywood. Four years later, after appearing in a few other TV shows, she makes her final small screen appearance in *Leave it to Beaver*.

# M

**Marr, Eddie** (1900-1987) "Water Anyone?" (Water Dept. Worker); "Train Trip" (Ticket Salesman); "The Grass is Always Greener" (Traffic Policeman); "The Bus Ride" (Bus Passenger); "Found Money" (Carnival Barker); "Beaver the Magician" (Uncle Artie)

Marr was probably most famous for asking Jack Benny, on his February 8, 1948 radio program the question, "Your money or your life?" That is one of the most famous questions asked in any entertainment medium. His most regular TV work occurred on *Lux*

*Video Theater, Leave it to Beaver* and *The Bob Hope Show* (his last appearance on TV, April 1971).

**Mitchell, Shirley** (1919-2013) "Child Care" (Janet Wilson)

It's debatable whether Shirley Mitchell was best known for her work on radio or television. On radio, she worked on *Suspense; Yours Truly, Johnny Dollar; Fibber McGee & Molly; The Great Gildersleeve* as Leila Ransom (her best known part); *Amos & Andy* and *My Favorite Husband*. It was on *My Favorite Husband* where she struck up a friendship with Lucile Ball. She later guest starred on *I Love Lucy* as Marion Strong. She acted in a plethora of good television comedies but none of her TV roles lasted as long as her role as that Southern Belle Leila on *The Great Gildersleeve*. At age 86, Mitchell lent her voice to a *Desperate Housewives* video game. Her second husband was Jay Livingston, the man who wrote the lyrics to "This is It," the theme song for the *Bugs Bunny Show* series.

**Montgomery, Ray** (1922-1998) "Child Care" (Herb Wilson); "Long Distance Call" (Kenny's Father)

Life imitates art sometimes and Ray Montgomery is one big example of it. He broke into films after signing with Warner Brothers in 1941, just before America entered World War II. His first few films included *Action in the North Atlantic, Air Force, Captains of the Clouds* and *You're in the Army Now*. In 1943, Montgomery himself entered the armed services, taking a three year break from Hollywood. His career was gaining momentum before serving our country and upon his return, he literally had to start his career over again. He played small roles on TV for the remainder of his career, winding up with a final appearance on NBC's *Hunter* in 1990.

# N

**Nielsen, Erik** (b. 1945) "Wally's Girl Trouble" (First boy in library)

The year 1957 was a good one for Erik Nielsen. In addition to his work on *Leave it to Beaver*, he had two appearances on *The Loretta Young Show*, one on *Dragnet* and had a bit part in the movie *Slander* which starred Van Johnson and Ann Blyth. But after 1958, he no longer worked in Hollywood.

# O

**O'Malley, Lillian** (1892-1976) "Lonesome Beaver" (Mrs. Whitney); "Beaver Takes a Drive" (Woman)

An uncredited role in The *Plough and the Stars*, starring Barbara Stanwyck and directed by John Ford was Lillian O'Malley's first job in Hollywood. After that beginning, she had a bright future but only worked sporadically until 1960 when regular work came her way on shows like *The Rebel, The Twilight Zone, Leave it to Beaver* and *Alfred Hitchcock Presents*. Her last role came in 1962 on *Alfred Hitchcock Presents* at the age of 70.

**Osborn, Lyn** (1926-1958) "The Paper Route" (Newspaper Customer #2)

Popularity came early to Lyn Osborn through his work as Cadet Happy on the radio and television series *Space Patrol* on the ABC network. His roles in future TV shows were never recurring and he wound up his career with three films which were released after his untimely death in 1958 following brain surgery.

# P

**Parrish, Helen** (1923-1959) "Lumpy Rutherford" (Geraldine Rutherford)

Beginning her acting career at the age of five, Helen Parrish was the daughter of a stage actress and sometime film actress Laura Parrish. Her first film starred Babe Ruth with her playing his daughter. Parrish later worked in several films with Deanna Durbin including *Mad About Music*, *Three Smart Girls Grow Up* and *First Love*. She had over 60 acting credits to her name at the time of her untimely death due to cancer.

**Paylow, Stephen** (1949-2011) "Beaver Gets 'Spelled'" (Boy)

The Internet Movie Database is not the be all and end all of Hollywood research, one time *Leave it to Beaver* actor Stephen Paylow proves this to be true. He wound up his career with 45 acting credits, but IMDB only lists five. His first film was *The Silver Chalice* with Paul Newman and it was this film which helped birth Paylow's lifelong love for history and ancient civilizations. He appeared on *Rawhide*, *Gunsmoke* and many other shows in the 1950s. He left Hollywood but not before working in the dietary department of the Motion Picture Hospital as a teen. For the rest of his life, Paylow worked in the food industry either in restaurants or in the dietary departments of various institutions.

**Prickett, Maudie** (1914-1976) "Beaver and Poncho" (Mrs. Bennett)

Maudine Prickett was a very successful character actor with over 150 acting credits. She had multiple or recurring roles on numerous television shows. Some of the better known shows were *The Red Skelton Hour*, *The Jack Benny Program* (Miss Gordon), *Hazel* (Rosie), *Bewitched* and *The Andy Griffith Show*.

 **Q**    n/a

# R

**Randall, Tommy** (b. 1943?)  "It's a Small World" (Frankie Bennett's Friend)

Randall's only other appearance in TV or film was on The *Ford Television Theater* one year previous to working on *Leave it to Beaver*.

**Reynolds, Alan** (1908-1976) "Beaver Gets 'Spelled'" (Second Man); "The Paper Route" (Newspaper Delivery Man); "Train Trip" (Man in Train Station)

Name every television series in the 1950s and you will see Alan Reynolds in the cast of many of them. He worked regularly and included on his resume some of the biggest shows of the decade including: *The Adventures of Superman, Lassie, Alfred Hitchcock Presents, Dragnet, Studio 57, The Loretta Young Show, Wanted Dead or Alive, Wagon Train, The Adventures of Ozzie & Harriet, Maverick, Rawhide* and *Bonanza*.

# S

**Sanford, Ralph** (1899-1963) "Beaver Gets 'Spelled'" (Fats Flannaghan); "Broken Window" (Fats Flannaghan); "Wally's Car" (Mr. Garvey)

A nice man on set and off, Ralph Sanford played bit roles in scores of movies in the 1930s and 1940s, many of the roles were uncredited. He was a regular on *The Life and Legend of Wyatt Earp* as Mayor Jim Kelley in 1958 and 1959 and from 1955 to 1958 also played four other roles on the same series. He also enjoyed regular work on *General Electric Theater*. A rather large man, Ralph Sanford passed away in 1963 of a heart ailment.

**Schallert, William** (b. 1922) "Beaver's Short Pants" (Mr. Bloomgarden)

If you wonder how William Schallert could have over 350 acting credits, maybe it's because as of 2014, at the age of 92, he's still acting. His last role was in the CBS comedy *Two Broke Girls* in the episode "And the Not Broke Parents" (Elevator Operator). His most popular role was as Martin Lane on the *Patty Duke Show*. Schallert is one of only three actors without recurring roles on *Leave it to Beaver*'s first season (the others were Louise Lewis and Lyle Talbot) who also appeared on *The New Leave it to Beaver*.

**Scott, Joey** (b. 1953) "Child Care" (Bengie Bellamy); "The Garage Painters" (Bengie Bellamy); "Beaver the Magician" (Bengie Bellamy)

Of all the successful alumni of *Leave it to Beaver*, the actor who played little Bengie could be one of the least well know, and that is a shame. Joey Scott, after leaving the small screen and moving behind the camera, has been a very successful TV producer since the 1980s. His productions include *Growing Pains*, *Hanging With Mr. Cooper*, *Sister,Sister* and *All of Us*. And after *Beaver*, he also had a recurring role on *National Velvet*.

**Shearer, Harry** (b. 1943) "It's a Small World" (Frankie Bennett)

The man known for the film *This is Spinal Tap*, voicing 21 characters on *The Simpsons* and who honed his comedy chops on *Saturday Night Live*, appeared in the pilot episode of *Leave it to Beaver* titled "It's a Small World." While he didn't play Eddie Haskell, he did play the role that would later become Eddie. His character's name in the pilot was Frankie Bennett. Two years before landing a part on the *Leave it to Beaver* pilot, Harry Shearer appeared on *The Jack Benny Program* as a member of a club named "The Beavers." In an interview with Bob Costas in 1998, Shearer admitted he may be one of the few people in America who had never seen an episode of *Leave it to Beaver*. That's almost sacrilegious.

**Showalter, Max** (1917-2000) "It's a Small World" (Ward Cleaver)

Unknown to many fans, an actor other than Hugh Beaumont first played the role of Ward Cleaver. This portrayal only occurred in the pilot episode. Fans who have seen the pilot are thankful that Hugh Beaumont took over the role. Showalter was a very accomplished actor and had in his lifetime, over 100 acting credits, his last coming as Grandpa Fred in the film *Sixteen Candles*. He also worked in films with beautiful women such as Marilyn Monroe (*Niagra* and *Bus Stop*), Hedy Lamarr (*The Female Animal*) and Bo Derek (*10*). Showalter was also a very talented composer and pianist.

**Silver, Johnny** (1918-2003) "The Clubhouse" (Man on Bridge)

Appearing on *The Jack Benny Program* in the episode, "Jack Takes the Beavers to the Fair," Silver is the second actor from season one of *Leave it to Beaver* to appear in this Jack Benny episode, Harry Shearer was the other. Silver played multiple roles on many popular TV shows of the 1960s and 1970s including *Make Room for Daddy*, *The Joey Bishop Show*, *The Dick Van Dyke Show*, *Mannix*, *Ironside* and *The Odd Couple*. He also had two small roles in the Mel Brooks' films *History of the World Part I* and *Spaceballs*.

**Smiley, Richard** (b. 1946) "The Black Eye (Fourth Boy); "The Perfect Father" (Willie Dennison)

The boy whose father was the bane of Ward Cleaver's existence, at least for part of one episode, appeared only in the abovementioned two episodes from season one and did not act on television again.

**Snowden, Eric** (1888-1979) "Beaver's Short Pants" (Clothier); "The Bank Account" (Salesman at Abernathy Potts)

Not to be confused with the 21st century American traitor of the same name, this Eric Snowden, born in England, was a distinguished old time radio actor. On radio he was heard in *Escape*, *The Jack Benny Program*, *Yours Truly Johnny Dollar* and many more. He made his way in the 1950s onto the small and large screen where he worked regularly throughout the decade. His last appearance was on the Twilightzonesque series *One Step Beyond* in 1959.

**Sullivan, Paul** (1944? - ?) "It's a Small World" (Wally Cleaver)

Unless you've purchased the DVD for season one, you have never seen Paul Sullivan in a *Leave it to Beaver* episode. This is the original actor who portrayed Wally Cleaver in the pilot episode, "It's a Small World," later replaced by Tony Dow. This was his second TV role. He first appeared in the series *Official Detective*. He later had bit roles on *Bachelor Father*, *The Donna Reed Show*, *Father Knows Best* and *The Adventures of Ozzie and Harriet*. He ended his Hollywood career in 1962 as an uncredited teen in the film, *Don't Knock the Twist*.

**Sully, Frank** (1908-1975) "Beaver's Guest" (Cab Driver); "The Bus Ride" (Cab Driver); "The All-Night Party (The Drunk)

Best known for playing cab drivers in bit parts, doing so 16 times throughout his career. Frank Sully was almost as popular playing bartenders, especially in westerns. On *The Virginian*, his only long recurring role, he played Danny the Bartender. He played this role from 1963-1967. Frank Sully also had the occasional small part in popular movies in the 1940s such as the *Grapes of Wrath* (Noah Joad), *Some Like it Hot*, *Yankee Doodle Dandy* and *The Talk of the Town*.

**Swensen, Karl** (1908-1978) "Voodoo Magic" (George Haskell) "Train Trip" (George Haskell)

One of the most difficult parts to play on *Leave it to Beaver* had to be the father of the annoying Eddie Haskell. Not really. In life, Ken Osmond who played Eddie was a very nice person. You may be surprised to know Karl Swensen is best remembered for playing Lars Hanson, the lumber mill owner in Little House on the Prairie. Michael Landon had remembered Swensen from his days playing multiple roles on Bonanza. Talk about typecasting, in six different shows or films, Swenson played characters whose first name was Lars. His recurring role on *Little House on the Prairie* lasted until 1978 when he died of a heart attack. His character in Little House was also written to have passed away.

# T

**Talbot, Lyle** (1902-1996) "Party Invitation" (Mr. Dennison); "The Perfect Father," (Mr. Dennison)

His career began in the early 1930s and Talbot seemed destined to become a star. He had small roles in some early Warner Brothers films, and in the 1940s, was leading man in quite a few "B" movies, many of them westerns. He was the first Warner Brothers contract actor to join the Screen Actors Guild and because of that, he never worked for Warner Brothers again. Talbot was trained on the stage and his earliest work included a stint as a magician. In 1930, he signed a seven-year contract with Warner Brothers. He is among three actors in non-recurring roles on the original *Leave it to Beaver* who also had a part in at least one episode of *The New Leave it to Beaver* series. The others were Louise Lewis and William Schallert. He was the Father of future *Leave it to Beaver* actor Stephen Talbot (Gilbert Bates).

**Thomas, Lonnie** (b. 1947) "The Black Eye" (Second Boy)

At the age of one, Lonnie Thomas got his first taste of Hollywood when he appeared in the short film *Parlor, Bedroom and Wrath* which was produced by the famed *Three Stooges* producer Jules White. He went on from there to roles in films that starred Shirley Temple, Walter Brennan, Fred MacMurray and Joan Crawford, all of this by the age of five. Just six years later, Lonnie Thomas would see his last Hollywood role as Jimmy in *The Adventures of Wild Bill Hickok*.

**Thorson, Russell** (1906-1982) "It's a Small World" (Man with milk bottles)

In the *Leave it to Beaver* pilot, Russell Thorson appeared as the "man with milk bottles." He was very busy about the time he filmed this pilot episode. He also appeared in three "B" movies and 7 other television shows during 1957. In the 1970s, he appeared in some of the best crime dramas on television including *Cannon, The Streets of San Francisco, Barnaby Jones* and *The Rockford Files.* Russell began his career in radio and played characters on *One Man's Family, Adventures by Morse* and many other shows.

**Turner, Patty** (b. 1949) "Party Invitation"; "Beaver and Poncho"; "Ward's Problem"; "Her Idol"; "Pet Fair"; "Beaver's Poster;" (Linda Dennison in all episodes)

As a child actor, Patty Turner was talented. She appeared on six episodes of *Leave it to Beaver* from 1957-1961. It almost seems unreal she would disappear from the Hollywood scene. She grew up In an acting family. Her younger sister Debbie Turner played Marta in *The Sound of Music.* Her family moved to Southern California from Canada for health reasons in the early 1950s. Patty still resides in the Los Angeles area.

# U

n/a

# V

**Vigran, Herb** (1910-1986) "Brotherly Love" (Stanley the Barber)

You may not know the name Herb Vigran, but you'd know him if you saw him. He was one of the most recognizable faces on the small screen in the 1950s and 1960s. He appeared regularly in multiple roles on *The Jack Benny Program, Dragnet, The Lucy Show,*

*Adventures of Superman* and *Four Star Playhouse*. Vigran was also a supporting actor on many radio shows during the 1940s and early 1950s. He died of cancer in 1986 and was active in Hollywood until that time.

# W-X - Y -Z

**Wade, Douglas** (b. 1949) "Music Lesson" (Thomas)

After his one appearance in *Leave it to Beaver*, Douglas Wade is listed in the Internet Movie Database as having played the part of a bartender in *The Return of Superfly* in 1990. It would be very interesting to fill in the missing years between 1958 and 1990. Look for more info in future editions of this book or in my upcoming *Leave it to Beaver* project.

**Wade, Stuart**  (1928??- ??)  "New Doctor"(Dr. Bradley)

Making his film debut in a short documentary about disc jockey Martin Block in 1948, Stuart Wade played himself along with his orchestra leader Freddy Martin. Wade was a very talented singer, the best ever employed by orchestra leader Freddy Martin. He also had roles in Broadway musicals before concentrating on film and TV. His career lasted in Hollywood from 1954 to 1964. In addition to a few TV roles, he also had prominent roles in horror flicks such as *Monster from the Ocean Floor* and *Teenage Monster*.

**Wagenheim, Charles** (1896-1979) "The Clubhouse" (Painter)

Debuting in 1929's *The Trial of Mary Dugan*, Charles Wagenheim's career lasted for fifty years. He died in 1979, still a very much in demand character actor, murdered by a burglar he surprised upon his return home from grocery shopping. His longest recurring role of his career came in *Gunsmoke* where he played Halligan from 1966 to 1975 in 28 episodes. Wagenheim was very active during the last decade of his life, with parts in 32 different TV shows or movies.

Among those were appearances in *The Six Million Dollar Man*, *Kojak*, *Baretta*, *All in the Family* and the movie *Missouri Breaks*.

**Warren, Katherine** (1905-1965) "Mrs. Brown" (Water Anyone?); "Beaver's Dance" (Mrs. Prescott); "The Dramatic Club" (Mrs. Prescott)

In the early 1950s, Warren garnered good roles in films such as *The Caine Mutiny*, *The Glenn Miller Story*, *The Steel Trap* and *This Woman is Dangerous*. Her first ever role was historic. She was in the cast of *Blind Alley*, a live televised 90 minute movie for WNBT in New York City, which was one of the first two commercially licensed television stations in the USA. WNBT later became WNBC. *Blind Alley* was one of the first commercially made TV movies ever.

**White, Yolanda** (b. 1951?) "New Neighbors" (Julie)

Not much is known about actress Yolanda White. Her first screen appearance was in the film *All Mine to Give* which was written by Dale Eunson who also wrote twelve episodes of *Leave it to Beaver*, albeit, not "New Neighbors." It is possible Yolanda White was a family friend or a niece of Dale Eunson. When more info is found out, it will be in an updated edition of this book or in my upcoming *Leave it to Beaver* project.

**White, Yvonne** (b. 1927?) "The Paper Route" (Newspaper Customer); "The Bus Ride" (Bus Passenger)

Most of Yvonne White's career was spent on the small screen, with a few exceptions being her minor roles in *The Best Things in Life Are Free*, *Bye Bye Birdie* and *Sex and the Single Girl*. That final film also included roles for three other *Leave it to Beaver* alumnae; Burt Mustin, William Fawcett and Max Showalter.

**Wilcox, Frank** (1907-1974) "The State Versus Beaver" (District Court Judge); "The Tooth" (Dr. Frederick W. Harrison, DDS); "Eddie Quits School" (Mr. Farmer)

A prolific character actor with over 300 acting credits, Frank Wilcox had a connection with Hugh Beaumont years before appearing on *Leave it to Beaver*. In 1952, Wilcox was cast in two episodes of *Racket Squad* in which Hugh Beaumont was the narrator. Before making acting his career choice, Wilcox worked in a lemon grove and ran his own tire repair store. But acting turned out well for Frank Wilcox, many honors have been bestowed upon him. Los Angeles declared January 11, 1964 as "Frank Wilcox Day," and also named him Honorary Fire Chief. Also, during the 1960s, Granada Hills, CA named him "honorary mayor." The final and maybe best honor to be bestowed upon Frank Wilcox was his hometown of DeSoto, Missouri honoring him on March 13, 2013 with their own "Frank Wilcox Day," and the First Annual Frank Wilcox Film Festival. Wilcox was a character actor legend.

**Windsor, Allen** (b. 1922? - ??) "The Clubhouse" (Ice Cream Man)

In 1952 Allen Windsor debuted on the big screen with a small part in *Scorched Fury*. After this film, Windsor remained dormant in Hollywood until his role on *Leave it to Beaver*. He finished his career in *The Purple Gang* starring Robert Blake in 1959, a very underrated "B" movie about a tough 1920s gang in Detroit, Michigan.

**Winkleman, Wendy** (b. 1948) "The Black Eye" (Violet Rutherford)

Wendy was one of the few experienced child actors on *Leave it to Beaver*'s first season who did not have a recurring role. She actually had about the same experience as both Jerry Mathers and Ken Osmond and had more experience than Tony Dow, Jeri Weil, Stanley Fafara and Rusty Stevens. Even with that experience, she did not come back to play Violet Rutherford in Violet's next four appearances in the series. Wendy went on to do more TV, but her career ended by 1966. Her brother Michael played Luke McCoy on the ABC series *The Real McCoys*.

**Wright, Will** (1894-1962) "Child Care" (Pete at Firehouse #7)

A former San Francisco newspaper reporter, Will Wright decided to switch careers and eventually made his way to Hollywood where he wound up with over 200 acting credits. He first worked with *Leave it to Beaver* writers Joe Connelly and Bob Mosher on the *Amos n' Andy Show* in the episode "Counterfeiters Rent Basement." He also worked on that episode with future *Leave it to Beaver* actor John Hoyt ("Part-Time Genius," "Wally's New Suit," "Beaver's Accordion"). Will died of cancer in Hollywood at the age of 68.

## About the Author

In addition to writing about God and a Beaver, young adult novels, children's picture books and ministry books, Brian Humek is also an accomplished photographer. His photographs have been featured in *American Cowboy Magazine*, *The Financial Times* and smaller periodicals throughout the world.

Brian has worked in ministry for the past ten years, first as a young adult minister in the churches of Christ, then as a non-denominational church planter and currently as minister for the Heartland Assisted Living Center church in Bedford, TX.

When not writing, Brian spends his time homeschooling his son, walking the University of Dallas campus, dreaming about the day the Chicago Cubs will win the World Series and watching *Leave it to Beaver* on Netflix and MeTV.

Brian lives in Texas with his beautiful bride, his very talented son and their rescue cat Wally.

*Final Note*

*Please remember to leave a review of this book on Amazon.com,
Goodreads.com or on your own blog or website.*

*Thank you.*

Made in the USA
Middletown, DE
08 September 2020

17721365R10099